Truth of our Faith is a book  nore. James Killian takes a refreshing ap............. is both easy to grasp and intriguing to yo..., and old audiences alike. Impressively, Killian is able to write from a completely objective perspective on the controversial topic; presenting pure fact in place of opinionated preaching. "Killian allows the reader to follow his research to examine the arguments he provides for themselves. In a day and age where anti-Christianity in youth has become a fad, this book is able to clear away some of the doubt and animosity people feel towards Christianity due to the falsehoods and lack of information presented." This book is perfect for any reader whether it is a student interested in religion or questioning the choice they have made; or a teacher or avid reader looking for an interesting reference book full of information seldom given in similar books. As both a student interested in learning more about all religions, and an agnostic individual I would recommend this book to any and every person I encounter.

Sincerely, Ashley M. Anderson

Truth of our Faith is worth the read. The way James Killian approaches his subject is objective. Although he is a religious man he is able to approach his own religious text in a manner that some might see as agnostic. However, "James Killian simply states the falsehoods others ignore due to their inability to see the truth without ones faith wavering. Using historical facts he weeds through the Bible and separates fact from fiction." As an avid reader and someone who has grown up in the shadow of the Bible belt, I would recommend this work to anyone interested in history, religion, or debating ill advised peers.

Sincerely, C.D.Harvill
Editor, Music, Art Trendi10.com
Nightlife Gulfcoastbands.com

Truth of Our Faith

JAMES KILLIAN

iUniverse, Inc.
Bloomington

Truth of Our Faith

iUniverse books may be ordered through booksellers or by contacting:

iUniverse
1663 Liberty Drive
Bloomington, IN 47403
www.iuniverse.com
1-800-Authors (1-800-288-4677)

ISBN: 978-1-4502-9319-8 (sc)
ISBN: 978-1-4502-9320-4 (ebk)

Printed in the United States of America

iUniverse rev. date: 02/24/2011

This book is dedicated to my beautiful wife and kids.
Thank you for your support and patience.

"He who created us without our help will not save us without our consent."
Saint Augustine

ACKNOWLEDGMENT

I would like to thank the following people for inspiring me to write this book and to help make it possible. Thank you my Lord Jesus Christ for creating me and guiding me throughout my life. My wife Tiffany Killian and the three beautiful children she blessed me with, Jonathan, Jayden, and Addison, thanks for your love and trust in me. My father Jerry and my mother Penny Martin for believing in me and giving me the life I needed early on. Thanks to my pastor Susan LaSalle, for the hours spent on Bible study and inspiring me to want to continue my studies. My long time friend Ronsan Coleman, who I lost contact with, for introducing me to non-denominational churches. To my friends Ronnie Desplas, Page Harder and Tarah Chandler thank you for your support, and contribution. I would like to also thank my editor Juan Hernandez for the time he spent editing my book, and for helping me to develop it to its full potential.

Abbreviation

A D   Anno Domini "After Death"

A.U.C.   Ab Urbe Condita, "from the founding of the City Rome,"

BC   Before Christ

ESV   English Standard Version

HSB   Hebrew Study Bible

KJV   King James Version

MGNT   Morphological Greek New Testament

NASB   New American Standard Bible

NIV   New International Version

NKJV   New King James Version

NLT   New Living Translation

NRSV   New Revised Standard Version

NT   New Testament

OT   Old Testament

RSV   Revised Standard Version

TR   Textus Receptus

Introduction

"I tell you of a truth."
Luke 9:27

It was a late fall night in October of 2002. I can remember flying in the night, looking down through the clouds at a small town. The street lights were on making shadows off the trees that obscured the houses down below. I recall seeing a waterway and houses that sat on the edges on both sides. The moonlight was glistening off the water, and I could feel a breeze touch my face. I thought to myself, *I know this place!*

While flying, I suddenly heard a deep voice coming from far above me: "Jamie, I need you there." Before I had a chance to comprehend and reply, I noticed a small town approaching fast down below. I fell through the clouds toward one house in particular, like a bullet fired at a target. Frightened, I thought to myself, *I'm going to die.* My pulse quickened, and I held my breath for uncertainty. I have never been as scared in my life for I feared my time had come, and then came complete darkness and silence.

My eyes felt heavy and I could hardly see. But it wasn't because of the darkness; my eyes felt like they haven't been used in hours. I realized I had been sleeping, and it was all just a dream. I struggled to wake myself, but strangely still felt fear and uncertainty. Days went by, however I told no one of my dream. It was just another unusual and obscured dream, surrounded by doubt within its meaning.

One bright, sunny, day I visited my father and his wife, Ruth. It has been a couple of weeks since I had last visited them, although we were only a few miles apart. The mood in the house was calm and quiet, a bit odd, I thought. While sitting at the dinner table finishing my meal, Ruth shyly said, *"Jamie, I need to talk to you."* My father abruptly left the table, as Ruth and I were about to engage in a private conversation. With a sound voice she said to me, *"Jamie, I am dying. Doctors say I have eight months to live."* Ruth had been fighting cancer for several years, and the doctors were sure they had removed all the cancer cells. Years of continuous smoking proved to be more than her body could handle. The cancer had quickly moved to her liver, and by the time the doctors realized, the damage was done. *"Your father will need you more than ever,"* she said. *"If you can find it in you will you come back home to help him throughout this troubled time. I have accepted my faith and understand what will happen. The cancer will spread quickly and soon I will be unable to help myself. I want to die here at my home and need you to be here to support your dad; he cannot go through this by himself."*

My answer was, without a doubt or hesitation, yes, for there is nothing more important to me than family. After finishing the details of our conversation, I kissed them both and made my way back to my roommate's house. I explained the circumstances to him, and being the dedicated friend he has been for several years, I knew he would understand. A week after moving back to my dad's and into my old room, I went out for an evening walk to my favorite place, an old chair my dad had made. I sat and watched the water in the bayou. As the evening sun fell and darkness rolled in, I couldn't help but stare at the moon and the appearing stars. It was then that I noticed the shadows forming off the trees around the house and the moonlight glistening off the water. Suddenly, it all came together: Everything happens for a reason, no matter how strange it might seem. Ruth passed away the following August.

I have had more than one experience in my life in which God intervenes. I was always searching for answers on religion and where I stand on my beliefs. Years of attending different faiths and consulting with different clergyman have only led me to confusion and aggravation.

I never felt as though my beliefs fit in with any certain faith. I always felt as though the church was leading me in a direction contrary to what I believed was Jesus' message. The lack of understanding is what led me to my studies. My mission was to learn as much about each faith and where each faith stands with their beliefs. I became obsessed with the early history of Christianity and how it turned into the formation of the different divisions today. I finally found myself secure in my belief and thank God for giving me the courage and ambition to do my research with an open mind, without bias.

The purpose of writing this book is to educate people with the problems that plague the Christian faith. For over two thousand years, the faith was formed from the decisions made by church leaders, Roman Emperors, and revolting monks who wanted nothing more than to move Christianity into a new direction. The circumstances surrounding each new direction slowly removed a small part of the true meaning of Christianity. What we practice today is far beyond the intention of Jesus Christ. We are left to embrace what we have and strive to bring meaning back to the faith. Education and knowledge of our history are important for anyone who wants to worship Jesus and practice Christianity in the form Jesus originally intended.

As the book title promotes, everyone needs to know the truth of our faith. The truth was buried beneath two thousand years of church reform and became lost. But who is it lost to? Lost to those who claim to be Christians, but who do not know the proper way to practice. The truth was lost to individuals who were at some time religious, but lost their faith due to some personal life event. The truth was lost to atheists for refusing God and church due to a lack of faith and understanding. Lost is the meaning of the word Christianity and how it is perceived in the public's eye. The message lost through centuries of debates and social meaning. Lost but not forgotten, Christianity can still be found if you know where to look.

In this book you will read my theology on subjects that some hold dear to their heart. These are simply my ideas on what I believe the scriptures are saying; what I see as truth. You may or may not agree with my points. You will be exposed to multiple views on the same subject seeing the sides you may have never known. You will have a chance to decide where you fit with your own theology and ideas. All the truths you will read are verifiable facts about Christianity and beliefs; you may not like all that you read. All my resources are listed and there is a Who's Who listing in the back. This list will give specific detailed information on all persons listed within the book for further references and research. My wish for you is after reading this book, you will have the knowledge and faith required to be the best Christian you can. Hopefully you will be settling down with a church whose beliefs and practices fit your own, and you are comfortable with. Good luck on your search for the truth, I hope this book helps you on your journey.

Table of Contents

Note to reader, all quoted Bible verses are from the King James Version, (KJV) unless otherwise noted.

Chapter 1:
The Lost Message

"And the scriptures cannot be broken."
John 10:35

S ince the day Jesus died on the cross, the religious world has been searching for the true meaning of His life. Revealed were stories and events of remarkable historical accuracy adding credibility to the Bibles content. Years of careful study and translations have brought more questions than answers regarding Jesus' mission. The one question that has eluded and plagued Christians since that infamous day is did Jesus get His message out before rising to His father or did He take with Him more of what we needed to know? For years after His death Jesus' disciples carried on His message and continued witnessing despite the overwhelming fear of both persecution and death. What they were spreading was a divine message to lead us to the Kingdom of Heaven. Since then scholars, bishops, apostles, and scribes have dissected His known life and have read, rewritten and reinterpreted the scriptures to suit their overwhelming desire to understand His message. In a desperate attempt to interpret Jesus' life and message, churches have split and Bibles have been revised. Within the last one hundred years alone, the Bible has been updated with more new versions to accommodate today's culture and society. With each new division of faith and Bible version the message of Jesus has been distorted, altered and possibly concealed. In order to sort this out, we must start from the beginning to understand how it all began.

Translating the Bible

The source of all Christian questions has come from the Bible, which ironically should be the source of all the answers. All the knowledge we have acquired about Jesus and His stories of divinity has come from the Bible. As practicing Christians our lives are based on the teachings found within the Bible. Such an important book, the basic foundation of Christian belief should be rock solid. But how exactly did this book come to be, and what problems exist to support the accuracy of the translation? The events of the Old Testament were thousands of years old before any civilization understood the importance of documenting the events. A good example of this can be found in the Old Testament book of Ruth.

Ruth 4:7, *"Now this was the manner in former time of Israel concerning redeeming and concerning changed, for to confirm all things; a man plucked off his shoe, and gave it to his neighbor: and this was a testimony in Israel."*

The author clearly felt the need to explain an ancient custom to the reader. Scholars date the book of Ruth as far back as 900B.C.

Another example can be found in Genesis.

Genesis 6:4, *"There were giants in the earth in those days."*

The book of Genesis was believed to have been written around 1500 B.C. The event written about took place hundreds if not thousands of years before. The first nine chapters of Genesis record the genealogy from Adam to Abraham and consist of thirteen thousands years of existed history before anything was written down. What was eventually written were stories of ancient events passed down orally from one generation to the next. Even from the original story to the first written account the culture and language had been changed. As stories generally are these were probably embellished and made more elaborate in order to give a deeper meaning to the events. All the books of the Old Testament were originally written in Hebrew except some brief portions which are in the Aramaic language (**Ezekiel 4:8-6:18, 7:12-26, Jeremiah 10:11,** and **Daniel 2:4-7:28.**) The writings of these books spanned many of generations and were rewritten throughout the ages. In Hebrew writing there is no spacing, no vowels, and no punctuation, just long continuous sentences. There are also no capital letters just lower case letters throughout the text. To make matters worse, you read Hebrew from right to left instead of the traditional left to right. For demonstration purposes the following verses will compare the KJV Bible to the Hebrew Study Bible. The verse numbers were left in to provide directional reading.

Genesis 1:26, *"And God said, Let us make man in our image, after our likeness: and let them have dominion over the fish of the sea, and over the fowl of the air, and over the cattle, and over all the earth, and over every creeping thing that creepeth upon the earth."*

Genesis 1:26-28 (HSB)

26 וַיֹּאמֶר אֱלֹהִים נַעֲשֶׂה אָדָם בְּצַלְמֵנוּ כִּדְמוּתֵנוּ וְיִרְדּוּ בִדְגַת הַיָּם וּבְעוֹף הַשָּׁמַיִם וּבַבְּהֵמָה וּבְכָל־הָאָרֶץ וּבְכָל־הָרֶמֶשׂ הָרֹמֵשׂ עַל־הָאָרֶץ: 27 וַיִּבְרָא אֱלֹהִים אֶת־הָאָדָם בְּצַלְמוֹ בְּצֶלֶם אֱלֹהִים בָּרָא אֹתוֹ זָכָר וּנְקֵבָה בָּרָא אֹתָם: 28 וַיְבָרֶךְ אֹתָם אֱלֹהִים וַיֹּאמֶר לָהֶם אֱלֹהִים פְּרוּ וּרְבוּ וּמִלְאוּ אֶת־הָאָרֶץ וְכִבְשֻׁהָ וּרְדוּ בִּדְגַת הַיָּם וּבְעוֹף הַשָּׁמַיִם וּבְכָל־חַיָּה הָרֹמֶשֶׂת עַל־הָאָרֶץ:

Eventually the Old Testament was translated into Latin, Greek, and Aramaic. As scribes began translating they eventually compiled a collection of copies upon copies. So large that it is believed that the source of the original text had been long lost. Take into consideration the hundreds of years of evolving culture and you can see how the text may have changed overtime. When words take on new meaning;

the messages start to take on new meanings adding to the confusion. Depending on the scribe's perspective of God, what one scribe interprets will be different from another. When translating to different languages you will find that many words have different meaning from one culture to another. Other words would have several different meanings depending on how they are used it the scripture. It was up to the scribe to decide which word was to be used in the translation. An example of this can be found in **Matthew 19:24,**

"It is easier for a camel to go through the eye of a needle, than for a rich man to enter into the Kingdom of God."

Some believe that there is a Greek misprint in this verse. The Greek word *kamelos* (camel) should have read instead *kamilos* meaning cable or rope, as you can see the words are very similar in spelling. In Jesus' spoken language, Aramaic, *gamla* means both rope and camel. It was from camel's hair that rope was primarily made. He most definitely uses *gamla* in his parable. It was when they wrote or translated Matthew into Greek that the misprint most likely took place, due to the two word meaning of *gamla*. Most scholars today believe the *Gospel of Matthew* was composed in the latter part of the first century by a Jewish Christian. Most scholars today also believe that canonical Matthew was originally written in Greek by a non eyewitness whose name is unknown to us and who depended on sources like Mark. However, other scholars today like Craig Blomberg disagree variously on these points and believe Matthew did write the gospels.

If this is accurate, as some believe, then the misprint or more accurate mistranslation kept ever since. In fact, the original Greek says *kamelos* (camel), not *kamilos* (rope). The latter *kamilos* is found in a few late manuscripts/lectionaries, mostly 11th century or later, and in one 9th or 10th century manuscript. The oldest manuscripts and a great bulk of the so called "majority text" are unanimous in reading *kamelos*, camel.

Still others maintain the stance that there was indeed a misprint. George M. Lamsa's translation uses the word "rope" in the main text, and a footnote on **Matthew 19:24** reads: "The Aramaic word *gamla* means *rope* and *camel*." It is noteworthy, though, that a *Greek-English Lexicon* by Liddell and Scott defines *ka' mi los* as "rope," but adds, "perhaps coined as an emendation of the phrase, *"It is easier for a camel to go through the eye of a needle than for a rich man to enter into the Kingdom of God,"* thus indicating that *ka' me los*, rather than *ka' mi los*, appeared in the Greek text.

For those that accept the Bible as infallible and reliable because it is the word of God, they have developed theories for the parable. The last two centuries have brought forth two explanations that are generally taught at Sunday school. There is a story of a gate in Jerusalem that dates back as far as the ninth century. A small gate called, *The Eye of the Needle,* located inside a wall that surrounds a town, only open at night and is just big enough for a merchant to enter. A camel can only pass through it after it is striped of cargo and crawls on its knees. It is meant as a parable about accepting Jesus. There has been no evidence of such a gate ever existing, no record of this design dating to that time. Another story is of a mountain pass referred to as *The Eye of the Needle.* A tight corridor thought to be impassable unless a merchant dismounts his camel. Again no evidence have been found of such a pass existing.

It is hard enough to understand the parables without any possible misprints and understanding the various word usages.

Early translation proved quite problematic. Through time words have lost meaning while others no longer applied. Some words do not have a translated counterpart, and therefore cannot be used. It then becomes impossible for a sentence to be translated correctly word for word from one language to another. When ancient scribes were translating words with obsolete meaning or no counterpart they had to read the entire verse word for word. Then they had to write the translation to the best of their ability and education to properly capture the meaning. When a scribe translates he also has to take into account both to whom and what language he is writing. The time period they are in, the ruling empire and the events they are dealing with also affected the choice of words used during translation. When writing for a city with a unique dialect and culture words may have been changed intentionally to accommodate their understanding.

Transliteration verse Translation

Transliteration is the mapping from one system of writing into another system either word by word or letter by letter. It is an attempt to reconstruct the original spelling of otherwise unknown words. It is not to be confused with transcription which maps the sounds of one language to the best script of another language. Translation is simply converting a sentence with the same meaning into another language without losing the integrity of the message. As a Bible student it is important to understand the difference. I myself had a hard time understanding the strange and unusual messages that are found throughout the Bible. It was with the help of a concordance that the message was made clearer. Throughout the transliteration process words that seem out of place were added to the Bible.

Unicorn s in the Bible

Words like *unicorn* stick out in a supposedly historically accurate book. In **Numbers 23:22** we see,

"God brought them out of Egypt; he had as it were the strength of a unicorn."

The transliteration word for *unicorn* is רְאֵם, *rĕ'em* pronounced as reh·ām'. It is a masculine noun and the exact meaning of the word is not known. Many believe that it is in reference to the aurochs. Aurochs or urus was a great black bull that inhabited Europe, Asia and North Africa. There are prehistoric paintings of this larger bull on cave walls next to bison and mammoths throughout Europe. It was very wild and untamable and was recognized for its brute force and power. It survived in Europe until 1627. I agree with most, that it was the auroch that was the inspiration of the word reh·ām'. Evidence does support this theory considering the auroch was alive and living at the same time the KJV Bible was finished in 1611. The translators of the KJV Bible were following both the Greek Septuagint (monokeros) and the Latin (unicornis) and then used *unicorn* to translate the Greek word reh·ām', as a reference to a wild untamable animal. The blame cannot be put entirely on the KJV translators considering *unicorn* does also appear in the preceding Geneva Bible that was in print from 1576-1644.

In **Job 39:9-12** we read,

"Will the unicorn be willing to serve thee, or abide by thy crib? Canst thou bind the unicorn with his band in the furrow? Or will he harrow the valleys after thee? Will thou trust him, because his strength is great? Or wilt thou leave thy labour to him? Wilt thou trust him, believed him, that he will bring home thy seed, and gather it into thy barn?"

God reminds Job of His creation and the power it has. He tells Job it is useless for agriculture works. To describe this creature as an agriculture type animal it becomes feasible to comprehend the idea of a *wild ox*. Most Bible versions use *wild ox* in place of unicorns while translating the text.

Unicorn is not the only victim of transliteration. The word for hare תבנרא 'arnebeth, pronounced as ar·neh'·veth, also is of unknown origin and is probably in reference to another extinct animal.

Scribes and the Bible

Scribes spent most of their professional life in a scriptorium. A room in medieval European monasteries devoted strictly to the copying of manuscripts by monastic scribes. A damp candlelit room made tedious working conditions not suitable for everyone. Their job was to rewrite copies of books word for word every day. Over time this repetitive work proved harmful to the meaning of the scriptures. Scribes not only have to perfectly copy entire books but they also had to maintain the accuracy of each copy. Misspelled words were common as were using words incorrectly and out of context. Add several misspelled words and incorrect word usage altered the message the scripture was originally intended to deliver.

Erasmus, a Catholic priest and theologian from the sixteenth century, acknowledges the problems faced with early scribes and the error in their translations. He writes;

> *"But one thing the facts cry out, and it can be clear, as they say, even to a blind man, that often through the translator's clumsiness or inattention the Greek has been wrongly rendered; often the true and genuine reading has been corrupted by ignorant scribes, which we see happen every day, or altered by scribes who are half-taught and half-asleep."*-**"Epistle 337" In Collected Words of Erasmus Vol.3, 134**

Uncorrected and often unsupervised this pattern of revision had continued for more than two thousand years and has led to multiple books and gospels about Jesus and His life. If an early Christian writer wanted his work to be considered as originally inspired by God he would often titled it after an already established author. It was common to see completely different manuscripts with the titles; Gospel of Mark, Gospel of Luke, and Gospel of Matthew, but written by someone else. Eventually there were hundreds if not thousands of books written in Hebrew, Aramaic, Greek, Latin and Coptic languages. With so many books floating around, it became a challenge for the early church to differentiate books written by the apostles and those written by men and other churches passing themselves off as men of God. The early church had the daunting task of weeding out false gospels using their knowledge of history, language and content that made each book unique. The entire Christian Bible was eventually assembled with these books pulled together collectively over time. It was not until Pope Damasus during the Council of Rome in 382 A.D. that the Biblical canon was solidified. The Council of Carthage in 397 A.D. convened to reconfirm the canon as set forth by Pope Damasus.

When one starts to learn and understand why and how our Bible came to be it becomes hard to pass the Bible as strictly the word of God, when history proves that the Bible is the word of men who were considered as inspired by God.

B.C, A.D.

The most common way of dating early Christian history is by separating events into B.C., (Before Christ) and A.D., (Anno Domini.) Both are designations used to number the years in the Julian and Gregorian calendars. But most ordinary Christians do not know that A.D. does not mean *"After Death."* Anno Domini Nostri Iesus Christi is Medieval Latin, it means, *"In the Year of our Lord Jesus Christ."* In simpler terms A.D. is recognized as, *"Anno Domini"* and begins with the birth year of Jesus. Developed in 525 A.D. by Dionysius Exiguus, under orders of Pope St. John 1, it was originally used to compute the date of the Easter festival, not to date any historical events. It was to replace a table used during the Dioceletian era, which was named after a tyrant who persecuted Christians. The Dioceletian table ended with 247 and was immediately followed by the new 532 A.D. table. Anno Domini is commonly referred to as Christian era abbreviated as C.E. both Common Era and Current Era, abbreviated as CE, are used by those who desire a term that is not associated with the Christian conception of time and dating.

Before B.C., Biblical dating

Before the B.C., A.D. system was developed, the only way for early Christians and before to the date time was to reference the year reign of the consuls who held office the year during the specific event. In the Bible this way of referencing is used more than two hundred times. Some examples are;

1 Chronicles 26:31, *"In the fortieth year of the reign of David they were sought for, and there were found among them mighty men of valour at Jazer of Gilead."*

2 Chronicles 15:10, *"So thy gathered themselves together at Jerusalem in the third month, in the fifteenth year of the reign of Asa."*

Jeremiah 1:2, *"To whom of the Lord came in the days of Josiah the son of Amon king of Judah, in the thirteenth year of his reign."*

Daniel 8:1, *"In the third year of the reign of king Belshazzar a vision appeared unto me, even unto me Daniel, after that which appeared unto me at the first."*

And Luke 3:1,*"And now in the fifteenth year of the reign of Tiberius Caesar, Pontius Pilate being governor of Judaea, and Herod being tetrarch of Galilee, and his brother Philip tetrarch of Ituraea and the region of Trachonitis, and Lysanias the tetrarch of Abilene."*

Further research reveals that the year of reign mentions coincides with other specific text written within the books. This ability to check and cross references events gives further credibility to the materials mentioned, and leaves little doubt about the accuracy and integrity of the authors.

The other more widely used way of dating was the A.U.C. system. This form of dating was used through all of Rome as a way of keeping the various regions in check with each other. A.U.C. means *ab urbe condita*, *"from the founding of the City Rome,"* traditionally set as 753 B.C. Some modern historians used A.U.C. as a way of dating specific events in Rome. The birth of Jesus would have been about 753 A.U.C. and the year 2010 would compare to 2763 A.U.C.

Birth Year of Jesus

Considering it is the year of the Lord. You may think 1 A.D., as the birth day of Jesus, but more accepted by both theologians and church historians is somewhere between 6-4 B.C. Biblical text from both Matthew and Luke reveals historical events and names of ruling authority that gives us a good understanding of when Jesus was born.

We know from Matthew that Jesus was born during the time of King Herod. **Matthew 2:1**, *"Now when Jesus was born in Bethlehem of Judea in the days of Herod the king."*

King Herod died November 27, 4 B.C. The Kingdom went to his son Archelaus who ruled until he was banished in 6 A.D. Luke also named King Herod in his historic account of Jesus' birth.

Luke 1:5, *"There was in the days of Herod, the king of Judea."*

Luke goes further into details by mentioning Augustus' famous census.

Luke 2:1-2, *"And it came to pass in those days, that there went out a decree from Caesar Augustus, that all the world should be taxed. (And this taxing was first made when Cyrenius was governor of Syria.)"*

The census, (taxing), is the key detail used to narrow down the possible date of Jesus' birth. We know that Caesar Augustus, who reigned from 44 B.C.to his death in 15 A.D., ordered three censuses to be conducted for all the Roman Empire. He listed them in *Res Gestae*, (The Deeds of Augustus). In 14 A.D Augustus carefully listed what he believed to be his thirty-five best accomplishments. The censuses are listed as 28 B.C, 8 B.C., and 14 A.D. There is evidence that shows several smaller, localized censuses for various reason of taxation were ordered by Augustus around 2 B.C and 6 A.D. It is however the verse that mentions Cyrenius as governor of Syria that has puzzled historians for centuries. If it was the one done in 6 A.D., *(when Cyrenius was governor of Syria)* that means Mary was pregnant for ten years. Obviously one cannot be with child for ten years, so how do we explain what seems like impossibility? We have to examine all Biblical evidence and key words. One key word to help solve this dilemma is the word *first*. *"This was the first census taken while Cyrenius was governor of Syria."* The word first clearly implies that there was more than one census taken. It could also imply that Cyrenius was governor of Syria during another term. Some Christian scholars try to make sense of Cyrenius title by understanding the Greek word used for the translation of Governor in the verse. Luke doesn't use the official title for Governor, "legatus." Instead he uses ἡγεμονεύω, "hēgemoneuō" which has a broader meaning. It is a verb meaning; to be leader, to lead the way, to rule or command as proconsul or procurator. Luke does not use the noun form ἡγεμών, "hēgemōn" which means; a guide, prefect, chief, sovereign, and governor. We can assume that since Luke was a historian that he was well aware of the different word usage and accurate in both his knowledge and history of the empire. Luke wrote for the understanding of his audience, the Greek-speaking population of the region. We know historically the Cyrenius held several position under Augustus such as; Governor of Crete and Cyrene in 14 B.C., Consul in 12 B.C., High Commissioner in 7-6 B.C., Legate of Galatia 5-3 B.C., Rector to Augustus's grandson Gaius in 1 A.D., and Legate to Syria in 6 A.D. Roman inscriptions found in Antioch mention Cyrenius as both legateship in Syria and separately the infamous census of Syria. Another Latin inscription mentions Cyrenius as high commissioner or as advisor to Gaius Caesar around 7 B.C. It is now believed that Cyrenius was either Governor twice. Once in 7 B.C and in 6 A.D., or he held another position in charge of the census in 8 B.C., hence it was his *first* census. It is more likely that it was this *first* census that Luke was alluding to.

After the banishment of Herod Archelaus in 6 A.D. Iudaea Province came under direct Roman government control. It had been part of the Roman Empire since 63 B.C. when Rome intervenes to settle a family dispute. In 37 B.C. Augustus made Herod, the son of Antipater, King and Syria was considered as an Eastern Province of the Roman Empire. It was in 6 A.D., that Augustus appointed Cyrenius as Legate of Syria to conduct a census in the Iudea Province for taxation. Josephus writes in **17.13.5** of The Antiquity of the Jews,

> *"So Archelaus' country was laid to the province of Syria;*
> *and Cyrenius , one that had been consul, was sent by*

Caesar to take account of people's in Syria, and to sell the house of Archelaus."

This assessment unsettled the Jews who resented the additional 5% tax imposed on top of the taxes that already burden them. It is mentioned in **Acts 5:37,**

"After this man rose up Judas of Galilee in the days of the taxing, and drew away much people after him."

With these historical facts in mind we can reasonably rule out the census of 6 A.D. as the time in which Jesus was born and being the census in Luke's gospel. Matthew's gospel further defends this notion because Joseph, Mary and Jesus were still in Egypt during the reign of Archelaus.

Matthew 2:22, *"But when he heard that Archelaus did reign in Judea in the room of his father Herod, he was afraid to go thither."*

The earliest possible date of their return would have been late 4-3 B.C.

In regard to Jesus' birth it was believed by King Herod that Jesus was at the most two years of age during the time the census was taking place. **Matthew 2:16,** *"And slew all the children that were in Bethlehem, and in all the coasts thereof, from two years old and under."*

Together these historical events imply that Jesus was not just born, but already a young child when he first reaches Bethlehem. This gives further credibility to a birth date of about 6-4 B.C.

The Gospels

It is commonly accepted by some historians that none of the Bible authors knew Jesus, and that the four gospels were written within 70-95 A.D. The earliest known works from the New Testament are the letters of Paul, believed to have been written around 50-62 A.D. Some of the Epistle letters are also believed to precede the writing of the Gospels. Yet one must wonder why no one during his time wrote down the events of His life as they happened. His disciples must have been eager to remember Jesus and His message. After all, a person as important as Jesus, *"The Messiah"* must be remembered and His message preserved for all eternity. It is easy to believe that His disciples wrote down events they remembered and considered especially important. Some Theologians believe that the Gospel of Matthew was actually written by His disciple Matthew, partly because within it contains Jesus' Sermon on the Mount. It is believed that this sermon is the earliest known words of Jesus documented. Matthew was the oldest disciple and the timeline of his gospel about 80 A.D. means he had to be an elder when it was finished. Matthew started writing his gospel only six years after Jesus died, or about 43 A.D. Therefore, it is conceivable to believe that the entire Gospel of Matthew is an accurate record of Jesus, preserved by His disciple Matthew.

John is another gospel writer that theologians believe knew Jesus. To back them up, I uncovered the following information: It is believed that John was the last to write his gospel around 70-85 A.D. He felt that the other three synoptic gospels were lacking the divinity of Jesus, and failed to capture His life as the Son of God. John concentrated his message on the spiritual side of Jesus and tried to establish Jesus as the Jewish Messiah that was prophesized in the Old Testament. He writes in **John 2:31,**

"But these are written, that ye might believe that Jesus is the Christ, the Son of God; and that believing ye might have life through His name."

He was writing to Gentile Christians who were facing debates with the Jewish Community while struggling to exist as a religion. When you read the gospel, it feels like an eyewitness account of the events in the last three years of Jesus' life. He uses words like *"and Jesus said"* continually throughout his Gospel, as if trying to recall His message. In **John 21:25,** he uses *"I"* as first person narrative,

"I supposed that even the world itself could not contain the books that should be written."

He mentions all the other disciples but never mentions John the disciple, only John the Baptist indicating that he may be John the son of Zebedee, (the disciple whom Jesus loved). John died peacefully in 100 A.D. while living in exile on the small island of Patmos in the Egean Sea, as a prisoner *"for the testimony of Jesus Christ."* John was the last disciple to die and the only one to die a natural death. It is believed that he wrote the Book of Revelation around 96 A.D. It must have taken him years to completely document his visions and compile the events together. Recent evidence suggests that the Gospel of John may have been published earlier around 50-60 A.D. due to the content of his message. There is no account about the Fall of Jerusalem in 70 A.D. He also never mentions the death of his elder brother James by the hands of Herod in 62 A.D. It is documented in **Acts 12:2,**

"He killed James the brother of John with a sword."

Luke wrote Acts in 63 A.D. If they are correct, being that John was the last to write his gospel that means all four Gospels must have been written much earlier than what was originally believed.

If traditional thinking is accurate, that is if all the books of the New Testament were written around 70-95 A.D. Then the only things the Gospel writers had to work with were verbal messages and stories documented by scribes. These stories were eyewitness accounts from His disciples. Luke credits them with his knowledge of Jesus.

Luke 1:2, *"Even as they delivered them unto us, which from the beginning were eyewitnesses, and ministers of the world."*

Do we really know if they recorded the message right? The contents of his life and his message must have been obscured in meaning. Hundreds of people were moved by Jesus during his time. He had to inspire them to search for the knowledge and keep His message alive.

Jesus' Lost Message

Jesus envisioned a religion based on brotherhood, peace and equality.

Matthew 12:48-50, *"But he answer and said unto him that told him, who is my mother? And who is my brother? And he stretched forth his hand toward his disciples and said, behold my mother and my brethren. For whosoever shall do the will of my father which is in heaven, the same is my brother, sister and mother."*

John 13:34, *"A new commandment I give unto you. That ye love one another; as I have loved you that ye also love one another."*

Matthew 5:9, *"Blessed are the peacemakers; for they shall be called children of God."*

Proverbs 12:20, *"Deceit is in the heart of them that imagine evil; but to the counselors of peace is joy."*

Christianity as we know it is most certainly different from the master plan that Jesus intended. Somewhere in the ages the message changed, not entirely in the scriptures, but mainly in the way we worship and practice Christianity today. Henry Tichnor writes,

> *"The message of Jesus struggled for existence to the fourth century, and then died, and has been dead as a door nail ever since."* **The Creed of Constantine**

The original message of Christianity can still be found; you just have to look through the endless clouds of faiths and Bibles that have polluted the church and obscured the vision of Jesus for years.

Lost Christians

There are many more Christians that do not understand their own faith and the history, than those who do understand. Try asking a faithful Christian that goes to church every Sunday and attends typical Bible study a question about early Christian history and the formation of the Bible. When you do you will hear answers such as, *"the Bible is the true word of God."* All they were told they need to know is in the Bible. Read and all your questions will be answered is what is generally preached. Christians have been comfortable with the title they carry, they do not think twice about the true meaning. They go to church, pray, sing and worship then go on with their lives until the following Sunday. They do not question their faith or their church's. These Christians do not understand why what they believe and practice is different than the churches down the road. These Christians probably do not pay much attention to the variety of different divisions of Christianity. They most likely feel that every church has a different name not a different belief system. They think the different Bible versions are just for easy reading and understanding not realizing the historical significance of their development. These traditional Christians are happy just being Christians. The Christians growing up today are different. They see the vast degrees of Bible versions, they see churches on every corner, they read about the problems within the Catholic faith, and hear about separation of church and state. Their brains are flooded with misguided information and the problems regarding religious faith. Christians today feel they have to take a stance on social debates that they never read about in the Bible. Are they pro-choice, pro-life, for or against gay marriages and the death penalty? All they know is that this is a Christian nation, and they are Christians. What does it mean and how does it affect them?

If Jesus were here today He would wonder, how we are all Christians, yet have so many different faiths. There are over one hundred and forty divisions of Christianity to date. It's no wonder so many Christians like me have a hard time discovering their own faith. With so many specific beliefs and practices, one would be easily confused and skeptical about their own. There exists a whole community of Christians that are desperately seeking church and religious guidance, but do not feel they fit it with any one in particular. If you are one, remember it is okay to have those feelings of doubt and insecurity; it is okay to ask questions about Jesus, life's meaning, and where we fit in with God's plan. God intended for us to make the decision on faith. It is up to us to read and learn the truth about the His message. We must discover for ourselves and seek the knowledge that will guide us in our understanding of God.

Matthew 7:7-8, *"Ask, and it shall be given you: seek, and ye shall find; knock, and it shall be opened unto you:"*

John 8-32, *"And ye shall know the truth, and the truth shall make you free."*

The Gospel of Thomas (1), *"and he said, whoever discovers the interpretation of these saying will not taste death."*

Proverbs 2:3, *"Yea, if thou criest after knowledge, and lifted up thy voice for understanding. If thou seekest her as silver, and searched for her as for hid treasure. Then shalt thou understand the fear of the Lord giveth wisdom; out of his mouth cometh knowledge and understanding."*

The Gospel of Phillip, Knowledge and Love reads, *"Whoever knows the truth is free, and a free person does not sin, for "one who sins is a slave to sin." Truth is the mother, knowledge is the father. Those who do not allow themselves to sin the world calls free. They do not allow themselves to sin, and knowledge of the truths lifts them up- that is, it makes them free and superior to all. But "loves builds up." Whoever is free through knowledge is a slave because of love for those who do not yet have freedom of knowledge. Knowledge enables them to be free."*

God gave us free will and with that we can decide for ourselves how our individual faith fits in with Christianity. We should not feel obligated to follow the church and the message the church transmits if we are uncomfortable with its direction. If we become dependent on church leaders to decide our faith, on what we should believe, and to learn about God then we are truly lost dwellers in life with no true faith of our own. Refusing to think for ourselves and make our own judgments would be like following the black sheep to the slaughter. Anyone can practice their beliefs in a manner that is consistent with the message and still be a good Christian. Love one another, practice and spread peace. Treat everyone equally, love and worship God is what we were intended to do. Jesus would be proud to see that two thousand years later his master plan is fulfilled. Nations are working together and churches are bringing together different faiths to worship. A world of free men and women loving one another, helping one another without regard to race, sex or religion. We can see from Jesus' *"Sermon on the Mount"* in **Matthew 5-7** the entire message Jesus intended on us to follow. Jesus sits on a large rock on a mountain side near Capernaum around 30 A.D., delivering a lengthy sermon to a large crowd which included his disciples. The sermon includes The Beatitudes, the Lord's Prayer, and lessons on how to live an ethical and moral life. This is what Jesus intended. We are a long way from brotherhood and peace. In the *Creed of Constantine*, Henry Tichnor writes.

> *"Jesus portrayed this life as a preparation of a life to come. We must live as brothers now, in order to be fit citizens of eternity. It is passing stranged that so appropriate a preparation and social life should have been so pointedly overlooked by the church all these years. And now that the socialist are demanding this life on earth of justice and human brotherhood-demanding it even though there were no hereafter-they are called enemies of religion."*

Chapter 2:
Christianity Reformed

"For by one Spirit are we all baptized into one body, whether we be Jews, Gentiles, whether we be bond or free; and have been all made to drink into one Spirit."
1 Corinthians 12:13

For the first one hundred years, Christianity resembled nothing more than a religious cult. They were a group of devoted radical followers that worshipped a single God and a man that publicly proclaimed to be both the Father and the Son. Their ways of worship were kept secret and their views were disregarded as delusional and irrelevant. Paganism was dominant over much of the Roman Empire and the known world; the competing Christians were struggling to be heard. In 64 A.D. under the Roman Emperor Nero, Christians were heavily persecuted being blamed for the Great Fire of Rome. The fire started on one hot July night at Capena Gate marketplace near Circus Maximus, it destroyed nearly half of Rome displacing many of the residence. Under Nero it became a crime to be a Christian and the abolishment of the Christian church became state decree. Nero had them hunted down and murdered for their monotheist belief. In retaliation of the great fire, Nero publicly burned to death hundreds of Christians.

Tacitus, a Roman historian (55 A.D.-120 A.D.) wrote about the burning of Rome.

> *"Nero fabricated scapegoats- and punished with every refinement the notoriously depraved Christians, as they were popularly called."* **Tacitus, Annals XV. 45**

Suetonius another early writer comments,

> *"Punishment by Nero was inflicted on the Christians, a class*
> *of men given to a new and mischievous superstition."*
> **Suetonius, Lives of the Caesars, 26.2**

He wanted to set an example and demonstrate the consequences of having opposing faiths and ideas. While at the same time deflecting blame thrown at him, for a supposed conspiracy. Nero died in 68 A.D., but the persecution of the Christians reluctantly continued with Titus the future emperor of Rome.

Fall of Jerusalem

Since 66 A.D., Jews densely populated Jerusalem. It was the settlement of an overzealous group of Jewish zealots who were fiercely defending the Jewish temple from constant attack from the Roman army starting in April 70 A.D. The siege was complete when the Roman army finally conquered the city, leaving a slaughter of Jewish rebels in its wake. The famous Jerusalem temple was inadvertently destroyed from a fire that started during the battle. The emperor Titus felt much satisfaction with the outcome for he strongly believed the siege would abolished both the Jews and the Christians. The Christians under pressure parted from the Jews and had to defend for themselves and move on as a religion. Once the Christians were on their own, they had to establish order within themselves. They had to agree upon their understanding of Jesus and what they believe in and stand for as Christians. The events were unfortunate and belittling but actually contributed to the massive Christian movement.

Early Christians

In response to the overwhelming pressure and constant threat to their religion, early Christians took to the underground caves and catacombs of Rome. They performed their worship in ways that would not be recognized by today Christian standards. Candlelight vigils, speaking in obscured languages, and circle dancing were common along with reading and writing of their early scriptures. There was even talk of cannibal like behavior, eating of man's body and drinking his blood. They would make the sign of the cross when they came out of hiding as a symbolic gesture for being in God's presence, but without any words because the belief of the trinity, as defined by the Catholic Church, has yet to have been established.

In the early 300 A.D., Christianity was finally being noticed more as a legitimate religious faith but still received a lot of opposition. The number of Christians was growing, especially with the younger more open minded citizens of the empire. As their new religion was spreading through the known world, churches and safe houses were opening to the devout followers of Jesus providing a safe place to worship. The Roman Empire viewed Christians as a threat to their way of life. Roman mythology and paganism were slowly being replaced by a religion based on salvation. Christians were arrested, murdered, enslaved, and forced to fight as gladiators.

Pliny the Younger writes in a letter to the Emperor Trajan about his experience with the early Christians. This unique letter gives a valuable insight in how Christians were perceived and treaty early on.

Letter 10.96-97, Letters of Pliny

"It is for me an important point of responsibility to refer to you as Head of State, things about which I have questions, since you are the person best able to set straight my hesitations and correct my lack of information.

Actually I have never been present at an Examination (cognitio) of Christians, so I do not know what punishment is required or how far it is to be carried out. Nor do I understand the legal grounds for a prosecution, or how stringently it is to be prosecuted. I am not clear about prosecutions in respect to the age of the persons, whether no distinction should be made between the young and the old, and furthermore whether a pardon should be granted in cases of recanting, or if there is no advantage for a person completely ceasing to be a Christian. Or is it the name "Christian" which is prosecutable, even if not involved in criminal actions, or is that "criminality" is automatically attached to the name?

In the meantime, I now handle it this way with those who are turned over to me as Christians. I ask them directly, in person, if they are Christian, I ask a second and third time to be sure, and indicate to them the danger of their situation. If they persist, I order them led dispatched (= executed). I have had no trouble with this, since whatever it was they admitted or professed, I decided that their obstinacy and unyielding inflexibility should be sufficient reason for punishment. Some others who were virtually insane with this cult, but Roman citizens, I sent back to Rome for trial.

As I continue with this handling of the situation, as often happens, the numbers and kinds of incriminations are becoming more widespread. An anonymous List has been brought out which contains the names of a great many persons. I decided to dismiss charges again any on this list who stated that they were now not, nor had ever been Christians, if they repeated after me a prayer of invocation to the Gods, and made an offering of wine and incense to your statue, which I had brought in to the court along with the statues of the Gods, for this purpose. And in addition they were to formally curse Christ, which I understand true Christians will never do.

Other named by the anonymous List said they were Christians, and later changed their statement. Some said that they had been and then stopped, some three years before, some longer, some even twenty years before. All these reverenced your statue and those of the Gods, and cursed Christ. They stated that the sum total of their error or misjudgment, had been coming to a meeting on a given day before dawn, and singing responsively a hymn to Christ as to God, swearing with a holy oath not to commit any crime, never to steal or commit robbery, commit adultery, fail a sworn agreement or refuse to return a sum left in trust. When all this was finished, it was their custom to go their separate ways, and later re-assemble to take food of an ordinary and simple kind. But after my edict which forbids all political Societies, they did in fact give this up. I thought at this point that it was necessary to get information from two slave women, whom they call Deaconesses (ministrae) about the actual truth, by means of torture. I found nothing worthy of blame other than the blind and over-wrought nature of their cult-superstition.

I have therefore postponed further Examinations (cognitiones) and made haste to come to you immediately for consultation. This situation seems to demand serious consultation, especially in view of the large number of people falling into this danger. A great many persons of every age, of every social class, men and women alike, are being brought in to trial, and this seems likely to continue. It is not only the cities, but also the towns and even the country villages which are being infected with this cult-contagion.

It seems possible to check and reverse this direction at this point, for it is quite clear that the Temples of the Gods which have been empty for so long, now begin to be filled again, the sacred rites which had lapsed are now being performed and flesh for sacrificial rites is now sold again at the shops, although for a while nobody would buy it. So it seems reasonable to think that a great many people could be persuaded to reform, IF there were a legal procedure for Repentance."

Emperor Tragan response,

"You have done the right thing, my dear Pliny, in handling the cases of those who were brought to you under the charge of being Christians. But it is not possible to make hard and fast rule with one specific formula. These people must not be searched out, if they are brought before your court and the case against them is proved, they must be punished, but in the case of anyone who states that he is not a Christian and makes it perfectly clear that he is not, by offering prayers to out Gods, such a one is to be pardoned on the grounds of his present repentance, however suspect he may have been in the past. But anonymous lists must not have any place in the court proceedings. They are a terrible example and not at all in keeping with our times."

During the great persecution of Diocletia 303-11 A.D., Christian's homes were confiscated, their precious scriptures and books destroyed, and they were denied civilian protection. The persecution ended in April of 311 A.D. when Galerius issued the Edict of Toleration. This gave Christians the right to practice without persecution. Their precious religion seemed destined to fail, until a major turning point took place starting with the birth of a great reformer.

Constantine the Great

Constantine, the first Christian Roman Emperor, was born February 27 in the late 280's at Naissus in Yugoslavia. He was the son of a military leader and a Christian mother. He was destined to become a great leader like his father. As a Roman Emperor, he was expected to follow paganism. It is not clear how his mother influenced him, whether or not she introduced him to Christianity or left him alone to follow in his father's footsteps. He never really understood his mother's religion, Christianity, and spends many hours discussing his religion with the

Bishops. After all, why should he believe in this new religion based upon one god and just forget about the last one thousand years of pagan history and tradition? He spent his early career fighting many battles with competing empires. In 312 A.D., he fought the infamous Battle of Milivan Bridge near Rome. According to the Christian Apologist, Lactantinus, the night before the battle Constantine received a vision in a dream. He saw the Christian monogram the Chi-Rho and was instructed to paint the Chi-Rho on his soldier's battle shields. Eusebius gives us a different version. He claims Constantine looked into the sun and saw the Chi-Rho above it with the Greeks words, *"Ev Touta Nika,"* in Latin, *"In Hoc Signo Vinces,"* in English, *"By this sign conquer."* He then instructed all his soldiers to paint the Chi-Rho on their battle shields. He was victorious, and professed he owed his victory to God. On his return to Rome a triumphant arch was built in his honor, and they erected a statue of him holding a cross. He was so inspired by Christianity that he issued the Edict of Milan which finally gave Christians complete freedom for their religion and legalized Christian worship. The Edict of Milan made Rome neutral to religion; no longer was paganism the official religion of the Roman Empire.

Under the new law, he abolished crucifixion, and replaced it instead with hanging. On May 7, 321 A.D. he ordered Sunday to be the official day of rest in which all public offices would be closed. Prisoners would no longer be locked up in the darkened dungeons; they shall receive daylight. Criminal were no longer branded on their face, because the face of man is the face of God.

Genesis 1:27, *"So God created man in his image, in the image of God created he him."*

All gladiator games were ordered to end by 325 A.D., in order for Rome to resemble the capital of the new faith. As the Roman Empire made the change from paganism to Christianity, it did not take long for Constantine to take heed of the challenge of unifying a divided church.

Reforming the Faith

Constantine was about to face a new battle, not a war over empires, but a battle to bring together all the churches of Rome and reform Christianity. All the churches were operating individually, yet no two churches were alike. The problem that existed is that all the churches believed and practiced different aspects of Christianity. They all had their own scriptures written in various languages with various messages and meaning. They did, however, share the basic fundamental of Christianity that Jesus was divine and died for our sins. The bishops of the churches were wealthy landowners, and with wealth and position came power. Converted Christians looked toward the bishops for religious guidance, so it was in the best interest of the bishops to guide and lead the congregation in a direction that directly benefited them. This started an unfortunate chain of events that led the message of Christianity to slowly dilute into misrepresentation of the scriptures. The attending Christians only learned what the Bishops wanted them to know. Later, in the year 380 A.D., bishops actually forbade the reading of some gospels. This was the time in which the congregations were not allowed to own or read scriptures. It was projected that only a religious leader could read, interpret, and teach the word of God. The motives for these actions were probably politically connected, for politics was highly involved in religion.

The divisions started during the time of Jesus. In **John 9:16** which reads,

"And there were a division among them."

He is referring to the Pharisees who observed his miracles he performed on the Sabbath, which was a sin to work on that day. Some of the Pharisees accused him of blasphemy while others were at awe and began to believe. The Pharisees roles were as religious leaders among the Jews of Palestine. They adhered to both the written and oral law and were strict followers. They were the biggest opponents of Jesus Christ, and with their help, Jesus was crucified. Some Pharisees converted to Christianity and eventually became prominent church leaders, helping to pave the way of the new faith.

As early as 100 A.D., early Christians branched off into the Roman Empire and made settlements in the east and west. These early churches differed in both faith and practices it is noted in **1 Corinthians 1:10,**

"Now I beseech you, brethren, by the name of our Lord Jesus Christ, that ye all speak the same thing, and that there be no division among you; but that ye be perfectly joined together in the same mind and in the same judgment."

Paul also acknowledges the divisions that started within the early church.

1 Corinthians 11:18, *"I hear that there are divisions among you: and I partly believe it."*

Later in his letter Paul reminds them that we are one in the Lord.

1 Corinthians 12:13, *"For by one Spirit are we all baptized into one body, whether we be Jews or Gentiles, whether we be bond or free; and have been all made to drink into one Spirit."*

In Paul's letter to the Ephesians he pleads to the church to unite as one,

Ephesians 4:4-6, *"There is one body, and one Spirit, even as ye are called in one hope of your calling; One Lord, one faith, one baptism, one God and Father of all,"*

Ephesians 4:13, *"Till we all come in the unity of the faith, and the knowledge of the son of god."*

In Paul's letter to the Philippians he pleads,

Philippians 4:2, *"That they be of the same mind in the Lord."*

As the Christian faith divided off, they cherry picked specific events and stories, like a moral buffet, and formed their faith around them. They reinterpreted their meaning to fit their desire. The results were divisions formed from a division, within a division.

Cyprian of Carthage, (200 A.D. Martyr September 15, 258 A.D.) Bishop of North Africa described the early church as so;

> *"Each man thought only of increasing his property: among the priests there was no devotion, among the ministers no sound faith; in their works there was no mercy, in their manners no discipline; false swearing, evil speaking, and quarrelling were rife; many bishops became secular agents, and left their flocks in order to seek merchandise abroad, and were eager in the pursuit of hoarding money."* **Farrer, Paganism and Christianity**

Cyprian also makes note of the separate divisions of faith,

> *"Christ has declared the unity of the Church. Whoever parts and divides the Church cannot possess Christ ... The House of God is but one, and no one can have salvation except in the Church."* **The Unity of the Church**

Epiphanius of Salamis who wrote in the mid forth century also noted the various beliefs as held by the many different churches. This passage notes an outcome from the Council of Nicaea regarding the beliefs.

> *"They passed certain ecclesiastical canons at the council besides, and at the same time decreed in regard to the*

Passover that there must be one unanimous concord on the celebration of God's holy and supremely excellent day. For it was variously observed by people." **Adversus Haereses, Hersey 69,11,1**

Constantine feared that a divided and failing church would anger God and bring vengeances upon him and the Roman Empire, now under Christian control. He understood that for Christianity to be a great religion he had to bring together all the bishops from the east and the west. The church had to operate as one unit all in agreement, it was imperative for the continued growth of Christianity. Over 1800 bishops were invited to participate at the council. Only 250-318 arrived to discuss the matter at hand.

The Council of Nicaea started on May 20, 325 A.D. at the imperial palace in Nicaea, Bithynia (present-day Iznik, Turkey). The purpose was to solve the ongoing disagreement over the exact nature of Jesus in relationship to the father. The Arian controversy, as it was known, was an Christological dispute that began in Alexandria between the followers of Arius and the followers of St. Alexander. Alexander strongly believed that the Son was of the same substance as the Father, that being He was co-eternal with Him. The Arians believed they were different, that the Son was only a creation of God. The debate, was He the literal son of God or the figurative son? Was he born, created or begotten? The bishops argued about the translation they were asked to agree upon. They had to make clear the meaning of certain words because words had different meaning in different languages. Constantine's role was to only act as an observer; he did not vote on any issues or give his opinions on any matters. His job was to enforce the doctrine. It was the bishop's job to decide doctrine and the proper way to worship God. Constantine's goal was to establish a collective group of scriptures and an understanding of Jesus that all the bishops and churches agreed upon.

Agreeing upon scriptures was the hard part. They all brought with them their own scriptures and books written in their individual languages. They deeply believed in the message they contained. Compared to the sixty six books of today's Bible, there were hundreds of scriptures and gospel between the churches. These scriptures were rewritten from stories and events passed down from generation to generation. To accept anything less than their faith, they would have to admit that their scriptures were wrong. Even bishops of their time had egos; they wanted to protect their reputation, after all they were representing their individual churches.

A positive outcome of the Council of Nicaea was the development of the first uniform Christian doctrine. Settled on June 19, the Nicene Creed was to clearly define the church's faith and became another cornerstone of Christian history.

The Nicene Creed

> *We believe in one God, the Father Almighty, Maker of all things visible and invisible. And in one lord Jesus Christ, the son of God, begotten of the Father, Light of Light, very God of very God, begotten, not made, being of one substance with the Father; by whom all things were made; who for us men, and for our salvation, came down and was incarnate and was made man; he suffered, and the third day he rose again, ascended into heaven; from thence he shall come to judge the quick and the dead. And in the Holy Ghost.*
> **Schaff's Creeds of Christendom Volume 1**

If you wanted to claim yourself a Christian, you had to believe and agree with the Nicene Creed. If you did not accept it, you were not recognized as a Christian. At this time many converts wanted to be Christians, and were willing to give up their pagan past. Christianity was rapidly growing, gaining popularity as a religion and it was viewed as the *"in thing."* Claiming yourself a Christian held certain merits. For example, Christians were being promoted to high government jobs. Constantine wanted to remove all Pagan officials from the empire and replace them with Christian officials. The unfortunate outcome under the rule of Constantine is that it diluted the meaning of being a Christian. People were converting for the wrong reason. Not because they wanted to worship God as their savior, but because they wanted to be accepted as Roman citizens and seek the benefits thereof. They were expected to give up their Pagan past and worship one God as their savior, and they did willingly. The Christian faith started to lose its purpose as a religion to follow Jesus Christ. The developing Catholic Church continued to move the Christian faith into the direction of unintentional values and beliefs. The true meaning of what it is like to be a Christian was slowly being lost.

Some theorists believed that the bishops at the Council of Nicaea may have had an alternative motive that Constantine was completely unaware of. They all agreed that they should be acting together as one unit for the sake of Christianity. Some believe they saw the council as a way to create a collective belief system, a system that will control the direction of the Church in their favor. It was an opportunity to structure leadership within the Church and for the Church to gain power within the empire. Understanding that both Christians and government officials would look toward the Church for guidance, they would have the ability to control the belief and lead the Empire.

The Council concluded on July 25, 325 A.D. coinciding with the celebration of the Emperor's 20th anniversary. Constantine continued to support the Christian faith by financially contributing to the building of churches. He thus became the founding father of Catholicism and of the Catholic Church. He built the Church of St. Peter in Rome and his own, The Church of the Apostle. He also built churches in Gaza, Alexandria, Trier, and Aquileia. Practically all the Christian churches of the time owed their existence to Constantine. He also never outlawed Paganism, but he did try to eradicate them by closing down their temples. Being the emperor, he never received contention due to fear. Constantine rebuilt Byzantium as a much larger and permanent capital of Rome. He renamed it after himself Constantinople, and it was dedicated on May 11, 330 A.D. He built himself a great church, The Church of Constantinople (in present-day Istanbul.). There were no Pagan temples allowed inside the walls of the new capital. Constantine wanted to ensure that the development of Christianity would not be affected by a delusional and desperate faith. To further help the church, Constantine commissioned Eusebius to deliver fifty bibles for the Church of Constantinople. Together with the Peshitta, these are the earliest known Christian Bibles.

The Christian regime that Constantine constructed had a negative impact on the developing Christian faith. Christians were now being persecuted by other Christians because their beliefs did not agree with the established Catholic Church developed under Constantine. He made the Catholic Church as the only lawful church in the empire, only what they believed and developed as orthodox was accepted as proper worship. In doing so some Christians sects were killed or forced out the empire.

Constantine, now a Christian had to deal with the murder of his eldest son Crisps and death of his second wife, Fausta. Fausta accused Crispus of trying to seduce her. Constantine in a fit of rage killed his son, supposedly by poison. Constantine later discovered the accusation to be false and had Fausta suffocated. Another version says Fausta wanted to escape the vengeances of her husband and killed herself at Travini. Their names were wiped from the face of many inscriptions and references to their lives were erased from history. For his now realized sins he sought forgiveness through the Christian baptism. He entered his last campaign with the intention of the conquest of Persia. On the way he planned to be baptized in the river Jordan, the same as Jesus. His dream was not to happen. In the spring of 337 A.D. he fell ill. Realizing that he was about to die Constantine was baptized by the Arian Bishop, his friend, Eusebius of Nicomedia, just before his death on May 22, 337 A.D. at Nicomedia. Under Constantine's empire, Christianity would rise to be a dominant religion. Both Constantine and his mother, Helena, were promoted to Sainthood for their efforts to reform Christianity and development of Christian rites. They are both celebrated as major saints of the Eastern Orthodox every May 21st. There is no question that Constantine had major influences on the development of Christianity. Without his drive to reform Christianity, there would probably be even more division of the faith and the meaning of being a Christian would have been lost. The churches would have continued the debate over the nature of Jesus and it would have spawned a generation of confused and lost souls. We owe Constantine for his efforts and should be thankful that we have a church, no matter what division of Christianity we are.

Chapter 3:
The Gnostics

"If you say, "I am a Jew," no one will be moved. If you say, I am a Roman," no one will be disturbed. If you say, "I am a Greek, barbarian, slave, free," no one will be troubled. If you say, "I am a Christian," the world will be shaken."
The Gospel of Philip

Who were the Gnostics? That's a question that requires a long explanation. The word Gnostic comes from the Greek word *gnosis* which means *knowledge*. The Gnostic writers were mystical people who claim to have been taught by the disciples of Jesus and posses a secret knowledge of Him that no one else has conceived. Their religion dates back as far as 35 A.D., when a sorcerer, and spiritual leader from Samaria named Simon Magus started a religion base settlement in Upper Egypt. These mysterious people believed in a supreme being that ruled over all other gods. Simon's people called him, *"The Great Power of God."*

Acts 8:9-10, *"But there was a certain man called Simon, which beforetime in the same city used sorcery, and bewitched the people of Samaria giving out that himself was some great one: to who they all gave heed, from the least to the greatest, saying, This man is the great power of God."*

The Bible tells us that Simon was listening to Phillip as he preached the news of The Kingdom of God and the name of Jesus Christ to the kings. He then believed and was soon baptized becoming a Christian and accepting Jesus. He continued with Phillip wondering and witnessing the miracles of God. Simon did not have it easy while traveling with Phillip. Phillip believed Simon's heart was not right in the sight of God and that he was *in the gall of bitterness and in the bond of iniquity* **(Acts 8:21/23.)**

Simon's acts revealed the first connection between the Gnostics and the Christians. The Gnostics consider themselves Christians, and their religion was influenced by both Simon Magus and Mark. Mark was not one of the Apostles of Jesus, but he was friends with both Peter and Paul who were. Peter was considered to be one of the closest disciples to Jesus. He was part of Jesus' *"inner circle"*, and was the one who Jesus appointed to lead the other disciples. Mark received all his knowledge of God from his extensive traveling with Peter while preaching his gospel in foreign countries. For years Mark traveled with both Peter and John, spreading the good news of Jesus Christ everywhere they went. When Peter and John departed to Jerusalem Mark continued alone. Most scholars will argue that Mark wrote his gospel around 60-68 A.D. The only problem with that date is the fact that Mark was martyred on April 26, 68 A.D., or the eighth year of the reign of Nero. The siege of Jerusalem took place two years after his death in 70 A.D. Mark talks about this in his gospel and most church scholars believe that it was going on at that time or that he was documenting current events. You can read about the, *"Little Apocalypse"* in chapter thirteen of Mark's gospel.

Mark 13: 8-9, *"For nation shall rise against nation, and kingdom against kingdom: and there shall be earthquakes in divers places, and there shall be famines and troubles: these are the beginnings of sorrow. But take heed to yourselves for they shall deliver you up to councils: and in the synagogues ye shall be beaten: and ye shall be brought before rulers and kings for my sake, for a testimony against them.*

Jesus makes a prediction about the siege early on and it is Jesus' prediction that Mark was writing about. Another gospel writer notes a similar prediction of the fall of Jerusalem by Jesus.

Luke 19:41-44, *"And when he was come near, he beheld the city, and wept over it. Saying, If thou hadst known, even thou, at least in this thy* *day, the things which belong unto thy peace! But now they are hid from thine eyes. For the days shall come upon thee, that thine enimies shall cast a trench about thee, and compass thee round, and keep thee in on every side, and shall lay thee even with the ground, and thy children within thee: and they shall not leave in thee one stone upon another; because thou knewest not the time of thy visitation.*"

I personally believed that he wrote his entire gospel while he traveled with Peter through Rome. After writing his gospel Mark took a pilgrimage to Egypt. There he settles in Cairo in 48 A.D. There he wanted to introduce the new religion of Jesus to the Egyptians.

These new Christian Egyptians are known as Copts, which today make up 15% of Egypt's population. Mark spent years teaching the Copts the history of Jesus and His importance as a spiritual leader. Exactly what aspect of Christianity he focused on is unsure, what is certain is that his influence to the Copts will also link him to the Gnostic writers. The Gnostics wrote their scriptures in an ancient Coptic Language, the same language used by the Coptic Christian bishops during some of their ceremonies. You will probably never see this connection anywhere but here. Nowhere in all of my studies did I find anyone making this conclusion. Another reason that I feel this way is the time line of the Gnostic Gospel writings, about 100-300 A.D. more than 100 years after the death of Mark. That is more than enough time for his preaching to both be learned and studied by the Gnostics, time they spent writing divinely inspired messages and the knowledge they acquired as new Christians. Throughout Mark's entire Gospel he uses the words, *"He that hath ears to hear, let him hear."* In the Gnostic Gospel of Thomas you see a similar phrase used throughout, *"Whoever has ears should hear."* These similarities are too significant to be considered as just coincidence. In these verses you can clearly see Mark's teachings being used by the Gnostic writers. My last reason is the connection between Mark's church, St. Mark's Coptic Cathedral, and the location of the discovery of the Gnostic Gospels in Nag Hammadi, which are both in Cairo.

The true reason for the Gnostics disappearance can only be theorized. They most likely vanished after the reforming of Christianity by the emperor Constantine. Constantine felt that any Christian sect that does not have the Old Testament as part of their doctrine must be eradicated. This act would only prove to help the cause of reforming the Christian faith. The Gnostic's writings were considered unorthodox by the new Catholic Church. They were accused of doing the devils work by creating false scriptures to lead people away from the truth. The Catholic Church was concerned that the Gnostic's scriptures contained heretical messages, and would give a new unfavorable face to Jesus contrary to the Christian faith. The Gnostics, in an attempt to keep their faith alive and not forgotten, hastily buried their works in a large jar over 1600 years ago.

In December 1945, a member of the Al-Samman clan named, Muhammad Ali, discovered the jar while digging for natural fertilizer near a cliff by the Neil River in the city of Nag Hammadi. Inside the jar was over forty-eight codices wrapped in leather. Today these books are collectively known as the Nag Hammadi Library. The discovery of these books outraged the Catholic Church. They tried to acquire them but were unable to do so because they were in the hands of a private museum. Scholars flocked there eager to read and interpret the books. They were more concerned with the messages they contained and what mysteries might be uncovered than preserving the delicate ancient text. Early handling proved too much for some of the pieces and they quickly deteriorated. The messages they contained were lost forever. What they discovered would forever change the perception of Jesus and His known life.

The Gnostics wanted to explain their belief about Jesus. They tried to fill in the blanks about the unknown life of Jesus that was left out in all the other writings of the time. Their writings comprised of books with *"gospel"* in the heading, just like the gospels in current Bibles. But unlike today's Bible their message is considered blasphemy, for they reject our belief in God. They believed the god in the Bible was an inferior god, that there is a larger god, *"The Supreme God"* that is unknowable. They have a different understanding of Jesus from the Orthodox Church. We are to believe that our God is a loving, caring and forgiving God. A god that loves everyone equally and wants the world he created to be free of sin. **The Gnostic Gospel of Thomas** reads, Jesus said,

"Perhaps people think that I have come to impose peace upon the world. They do not know that I have come to impose conflicts upon the earth: fire, sword, war. For there will be five in a house: there will be and two against three, father against son and son against father, and they will stand alone."

In the Infancy Gospel of Thomas they fill in the details about His early childhood. They portrayed Him as a violent and vengeful youth who does not understand His powers or the importance of who He is. He miss uses His divine powers buy taking the lives of children, yet shows remorse by raising the dead and feeding the poor. Other outrageous claims involve the belief that Jesus was never here in flesh, but only appeared in flesh. In the KJV Bible you will read,

Romans 8:3-4, *"For what the law could not do, in that it was weak through the flesh, God sending his own Son in the likeness of sinful flesh, and for sin, condemned sin in the flesh: That the righteousness of the law might be fulfilled in us, who walk not after the flesh, but after the Spirit."*

It clearly reads that God sent His son in the likeness of flesh. We should follow only the spirit of Jesus and not His flesh. In the **Gnostic Gospel of Thomas,** Jesus said,

"Shame on the flesh that depends on the soul. Shame on the soul that depends on the flesh."

The Gnostic writers make a clear distinction between the soul, *"spirit"* and the flesh. The Son of the Supreme God could not live in flesh, because flesh is sin. They also reject the Bibles crucifixion story.

They felt that the Supreme God would not allow His only Son to die such a horrific death. In **Mark 15:21** you will read,

"And they compel one Simon a Cyrenian, who passed by, coming out of the country, the father of Alexander and Rufus, to bear his cross."

The Gnostics rewrite it claiming that when Simon of Cyrene stopped to help Jesus with the cross, he somehow did a body switch with Jesus. Simon was the one who carried the cross in the likeness of Jesus, and it was Simon who was crucified, while Jesus was standing behind laughing and mocking the soldiers for their ignorance. What I find interesting with Simon is that he is from Cyrene, a small city in north Libya, in North Africa, which is the same city that is the birth place of Mark the Apostle. The distance from Cyrene and Nag Hammadi is only about five hundred miles. The Gnostic writers used Simon as a way to connect their belief with that of Christian faith. What is even more interesting is how the Catholic Church recognized the events of Simon and uses the story as part of their stations of the cross.

This is not the only time in which the Gnostic Gospels either reflects or appears to back up claims in our Bible. Both of them talk about Jesus' youth in the temple studying scriptures with the elders and teachers. **Luke 2:46-47,** " *And it came to pass, that after three days they found him in the temple, sitting in the midst of the doctors, both hearing them, and asking them questions. And all that heard him were astonished at his understanding and answers.*"

Now compare that to **The Infancy Gospel of Thomas** which reads, *"After three days they found him in the temple areas, sitting among the teachers, listening to the law and asking them questions. All eyes were on him, and everyone was astounded that he, a mere child, could interrogate the elders and teachers of the people and explain the main points of the law and the parables of the prophets."*

Both consistently preach the importance of finding knowledge and of the mysteries of heaven.

Mark 4:11, *"And he said unto them, unto you it is given to know the mystery of the kingdom of God."*

Ephesians 1:17, *"That the God of our lord Jesus Christ, the Father of glory, may give unto you the spirit of wisdom and revelation in the knowledge of him."*

In the **Gnostic Gospel of Thomas** it reads,

"Know what is in front of your face, and what is hidden from you will be disclosed to you. For there is nothing hidden that will not be revealed."

From **The Hidden Sayings of Jesus** which reads,

"Let one who seeks not stop seeking until one finds. When one finds, one will be astonished, and having been astonished, one will reign and having reigned, one will rest."

John 8:34, *"Whosoever committeth sin is the servant of sin."*

The Gnostic Gospels reads similar, *"one who sins is a slave of sin."*

You will find numerous connections between the Gnostic's ideas and what is written in the Bible. Clearly you can see the intentions of the Gnostics from a Christian's point of view. It is hard to reject the idea that all of the Gnostic's writings were blasphemy. Some of their messages are written in such a mysterious way that it becomes hard to fully conceive their ideas and understand their message. Yet when you read you feel completely connected to their ideas like you just received the answers to your questions. The Bible, as we are taught, is the divine message of Jesus. To be believed, for within it contains the accurate account of Jesus' life and instructs us on how to live a moral life. Clearly the Gnostics had access to the New Testament Gospels for they were written from 48-70 A.D. Surely the Gnostics felt as though they too were divinely inspired when they were writing. To only accept the orthodox of the Bible and to not be willing to consider other ancient text is holding a blind eye to some truths about Christianity and the knowledge contained therein. I am not preaching the Gnostics belief neither do I condone them. You have to have an open mind to read the Gnostic Gospels and accept that the writers were convinced they were writing divine messages of Jesus. There were new insights about the life of Jesus revealed to us in discovered ancient text such as the Nag Hammadi Library and the Dead Sea Scrolls. Stories that shed new light on previous unknown events and of Jesus' early life and reveal to us the thoughts of Jesus by the early writers. Personally, I am convinced that there are some truths within the writings. There is a lot of knowledge that one can gain about Jesus and His message. One may even find peace with the idea that their belief and idea of Jesus is similar to the Gnostic's text. Believing will not change your Christian status, but understanding the text and the messages will surely strengthen your own faith in God.

If it were not for the Gnostics writing their belief, Christianity would not have been formed into what we know today. Their claims, whether true or not, forced the Christian faith to move forward as a reformed belief. We owe them for their ingenuity and determination for documenting their belief in the face of persecution and war. For more information on the Gnostics I recommend reading, *"The Gnostic Gospel of Jesus"*, by **Marvin Meyer**.

Chapter 4:
Atheists Lost from God

"The fool hath said in his heart, There is no God."
Psalm 14

L oss of faith and religion would be the wrong way to describe an atheist. An atheist refuse to accept the existence of a god or any supreme being that is creator of all. Yet some are able to practice other forms of religious faith. No one is born into atheism, just like no one is born into racism; it is a choice one has to make. Atheists chose to close down all emotional paths which lead to God. This is why it is common to hear an atheist say that God does not speak to them. They do not see Him or even feel Him, therefore by reason and logic He does not exist. For those that say they never hear God, I always tell them, *"Listen with your heart and not with your ears."* I continue with, *"Have you ever done something bad you knew you should not do, and you heard this soft voice in the back of your head warn you not to do it?"* Well that was God, and He guides you through emotion.

The reason why I want the reader to understand this subject is to clear the misconception atheists have on the subject of Christianity. Atheists have to learn their ideas from somewhere; they did not develop this misconception on their own without outside influences. Like peer pressure is a problem for kids it is a similar problem for atheists, wanting to be accepted by other atheists. The internet is full of anti-Christian propaganda. Most of which is poor and bias researched done by someone with a secret agenda at tearing down Christian values. Atheist and other none believes are easily influence on their ideas and before long they believe in poorly developed theories as fact. This is a huge problem with our younger generation. It is today's youth that are the most influenced and most at risk in believing these false and dangerous ideas.

Age of Reason

The seventeenth century French philosopher and atheist, Rene Descartes coined the phrase, *"Cogito, ergo sum."* "I THINK; THEREFORE, I AM." Part of the 17th century philosophy called the *Age of Reason* he helped to usher in a new era of modern philosophy and logic. Emerging from the Western world *The Age of Reason* set the stage for a radical political movement, one that openly embraced republicanism and atheism. Organized religion was criticized for its unnecessary rituals and doctrines, and it challenged the legitimacy of the Bible. Believing that all knowledge has to come through the senses and from experience, this new era taught citizens not to trust the Bible, but to use logic. The movement gained popularity in America when Thomas Pain fled here in the late 1790s. Here he finished part three of *The age of Reason: An Examination of the Passages in the New Testament, Quoted from the Old and Called Prophecies Concerning Jesus Christ.* Their acts set in stone the foundation that atheists rely upon for arguing religious tolerance.

Philosophy and science are two defenses against religion used by atheists. They claim that all natural phenomena can be explained without God. They feel that we all come from matter created over a billion years ago, and evolution is the only process that created the life that formed on our planet.

Of the world's total population about 12% claim no religion, of that only about 9% claim to be atheists. Between 64% and 80% of Japanese describes themselves as atheists, agnostics, or non-believers. According to a poll by *Der Spiegel* magazine, 45% of Germans believe in God, and a quarter in Jesus Christ. The percentage of such persons in European Union member states ranges as low as single digits in Malta, Poland, Romania, Cyprus and some other countries, and up to 85% in Sweden, 80% in Denmark, 72% in Norway, and 60% in Finland

Why do so many people make the conscious decision to refuse God? We will examine the reason and motivation why some choose their non-belief.

To first clarify my thought I want to let you, the reader know that there are two types of atheists. The first type and largest group are those that refuse to admit in the existence of a god and are just happy with that. They do not talk or engaged in conversation because to them, what's the point. The second and most damaging are those who sole purpose of being an atheist is to insult, ridicule and belittle Christians for their beliefs. I used Christianity because most atheists are ex-Christians. This group wants to argue and instigate debates on their views about Christianity. They take personal attacks at belief because their lack of. And it is this group that the rest of this chapter is about.

Every event in our lives shapes our outlook on life. The outcome of such events dictates the direction in which we take our life. This statement is true for everyone. Take 9-11-01 for example. Many of our nation's youth felt the need to fight and join the military to defend freedom; while many older citizens were against going to war because they have already seen the results of wars. Both age and circumstance play a major role and influences our decisions we make in life.

A true story
There was this religious woman, who wanted to have a child more than anything. After numerous attempts and one lost pregnancy, finally success, she made it to her third trimester and out of the danger zone. While her husband was fighting for our country in Iraq she continued her job in retail management. She lived by herself and was content with working the long demanding hours that her job required of her. Her mother and father lived in another state, and she had few friends to comfort her in her times of need. On a Wednesday night after work she was planning her day off on the way back home. Her plans included baby shopping, decorating, and some relaxing. That Thursday morning she received a call from her boss. The scheduled closing manager had called in, and she was needed to give up

her day off and work to close the store. The day was like any normal day, nothing she could not handle. I had a chance to talk to her regarding her pregnancy during my lunch. She seemed very excited yet nervous. She had just finished the nursery, and had a baby shower. She was making plans with both her doctor and the hospital regarding her expected delivery date, only weeks away. Everything was looking great; she could not wait to see the baby she had been carrying for the last eight months. After closing and locking up, leaving the night stockers inside the store, she got into her car and headed home. While driving home on the long dark road of highway 603, she received an alarm callback from the store requiring her to return and disarm it. Apparently one of the night stockers had accidently hit an emergency door with power equipment setting off the alarm. She stopped on the shoulder and proceeded to make a u-turn. Unfortunately, a young drunk driver had fallen asleep at the wheel. Half way through her turn he veered across the center lane hitting her head on. The combine impact was brutal. The young driver was killed, and she lost her baby. After two days, while in the hospital in critical condition she lost her battle and died from the massive injuries she had received. Sadly enough she was aware that she had lost her baby. The pain she must have felt had to have been unbearable. I can remember how I felt when I heard the terrible news and how it affected me. I did a lot of soul searching and praying, trying to make sense of the tragedy. My only conclusion was that God wanted her at that very time. Let's pretend the accident never happened. Everything was normal and she delivered the baby. What could have happened that would warrant God taking her? Maybe there would have been a problem with the delivery of the baby, or maybe with her. Since she had lost another baby due to a rare medical disorder, how could she possibly bear the loss after already losing one? What if something bad would have happened to her as a result of delivering the baby; some overlooked medical condition that could have been life threatening? What if she died and the baby had to go on living never knowing her mother and the father was left raising the baby alone as a widower; how is that fair for anyone? Whatever the reason, it was best for both of them to go together.

You can see how this dramatic event would change a person's perspective of the decisions and actions of God and question Him. A mildly religious individual would probably cast doubts on his or her belief in an all loving, merciful, and caring God. All atheists share a common connection. They all decided to refuse faith and belief in a supreme being, although their reason for doing so varies.

The biggest reason atheists refuse God is having their parents push their beliefs onto them at a young age. These individuals are forced to attend church every Sunday as kids, and live strict moral lives, and do not even understand why. At a time in life in which one hardly understand who God is anyway. A time in one's life when one is vulnerable to skepticism, confusion and misdirection. In today's culture everyone has access to the internet and the vast knowledge contained within. The problem with that is that the internet is public, open to anyone who wants to express their views. This has lead to numerous sites with biased and hate filled messages that contain false, misleading and overall damaging content. Content so intentionally construed that it becomes an easy influence on younger people who are seeking information and fall prey to other delusional ideas and beliefs without even being aware that what they are accepting as truth are based on lies or mostly lies.

Refusing God is a way of acting out, and a way to retaliate for being pressured into believing in a religion that they never understood. Atheists, by nature are nonconformists. A nonconformist does not accept church dogma or boundaries set forth by the church. They do not live within walls, but outside the boundaries in their own comfort zone. They are more comfortable denying the possibility than conceiving the probability.

When I was ten my father married Penny, my stepmother. She is a deeply religious person who converted me to Catholicism from a Lutheran past. She sent me to a private Catholic school, St. Rosalie elementary. We went to church every Sunday, and sometimes on Wednesdays. In junior high I became an altar boy for St. John Bosco Catholic church. I participated in all church activities including the youth group. At this time in my life all I knew was that it was a chore. Something I had to do. I never understood the purpose of structured religion. When my father and Penny divorced I moved away with my father and sister to another city some distance away. I had to finish my education at a public school. Yet I continued to attend church and made my confirmation. While out of high school, with no plans in life, I fell into a period of deep depression. I forgot about God and drifted into non- believing. My sister went in the same direction when she left for college, but sadly, she never regained her faith. I on the other hand, was stronger in faith. After meeting my friend Ronson, who was non denominational, I regained the faith I once lost and started to study God and His message.

Some atheists convert due to a negative experience with a church organization. I spoke to a former Jehovah's Witness about her past and why she is now Agnostic. She told me that one day she had wanted to join the Jehovah's Witnesses as they went door to door. After she had joined she went to the local Kingdom Hall where she was a member. She pleaded that she wanted to do something more, and wanted a bigger part within the church. She was denied any part of church services due to the sins her father committed. She asked herself,

> *"How can they deny me when all they do is push their beliefs onto others and try to get people to join their church."*

Feeling more than insulted, and disgusted with the church she made the decision to leave, in essence she disfellowshipped herself. She was quoted saying.

> *"A relationship with God is not much different than an "earthly" relationship. People may fall in love quickly and pour all faith and trust into another person without knowing every fabric of their personality. People may also get burned and offended easily and move onto another*

relationship or swear them off altogether. It seems as though people who "get back into the game" seem happier than those who spread their misery." **Erika Helms**

Many people attend church and question the motives of their pastor, especially when they hear the request for offerings. Why does God want our money? Is it really for the church? Am I paying for their nice clothes, jewelry, car or even their mortgage? Doubt and lack of trust within the church is far more than some can bear. What they are forgetting is that they are choosing to leave the church, not God. Unfortunately that is the final outcome when one has lost their faith in religion. They begin to blame churches and organized religions for the problems in society, ultimately forgetting that God, church and society are all separate.

Surprisingly non-believers and believers do share a common belief. We all believe that Earth is filled with evil. The believers define evil as Satan and sins. False prophets with false teachings and corruption against morality also give believers proof of evil. For non-believers evil is defined as; war, hunger, murder, natural disasters, poverty, and the political corruption that plague our planet. Non-believers use evil as their number one defense for not accepting God. The general census seems to be that if there was a God there should be no evil.

For some atheists it takes a dramatic event in life that had a negative impact to lose their faith. I had an atheist admit it took 9-11-01 for him to not believe. He asked,

"How can a handful of Muslim terrorists kill thousands of innocent people in the name of Allah?" "Whose side is God on, if there is one?"

I had other atheists asked me.

"If there is a God then why did this happen to me or him/ her?" "If God is all loving and caring then why is this

*world messed up?" "Why are people starving, babies dying,
murdering and killing of innocent people, war and nations
hating nations?" "Why does He let natural disasters like
tsunamis, hurricanes, and earthquakes happen if He is all
powerful and can stop them?" "If God knows what we are
going to do before we do it then why did He create us and
let us do it."*

There are no answers good enough to satisfy the anger and
resentment that has been boiling inside of atheists. No words of comfort
can make up for two thousand years of hatred and war that religion has
been blamed for. And you cannot tell them that God does everything
for a reason, for that kind of talk is ignorant making no sense to non
believers.

Experiment on facts

I secretly played out a public experiment on non-believers without them
being aware of my intentions on Yahoo Answers, Religion & Spirituality
board. I wanted to see if presented with historical facts if a non-believer
would accept them as truth based on what others told them or what they
learned on their own. I asked a two part question based on the early
history of America. I then waited for responses. What I found did not
surprise me. My question was,

> *"Do atheists ignore the historical fact that the phases, "Under
> God" and "In God we trust" were around prior to the 1940's?
> Why live in denial and ignore our nation's history?"*

Answers.
-*No, but apparently you do.*
-*You are wrong. Those were not originally there, check your facts.*
-*Not in the pledge, your argument is wrong.*
-*So history starts when you say so, nice.*

-The words "Under God" were added between "One Nation" and "Indivisible."
-Better check that history book again.
-"Under God" was added to the Pledge in 1956. "In God We Trust" was
adopted by the same time.
-"Under God" and "God We Trust" were added to the pledge and money
in the 1950's.
-You might want to check your sources. "Under God" was added to the
Pledge in 1956.
-No they were not around prior and you are the one making things up.

I have received over thirty responses most of which ridiculed my question. All the responses were the same that is; they immediately believed I was wrong without knowing proper American history and assumed I was in reference to the flag and paper money.

I want to give you, the reader some quick background facts on *"Under God"* and *"In God We Trust."* *"One Nation under God"* was first added to the pledge on February 12, 1948, which is Lincoln's birthday. Louis A. Bowman (1872-1959), who added the phase, stated that the words came from Abraham Lincoln's Gettysburg Address of 1863. All of the reporters present wrote down the entire transcript of his speech, and each one contains the words, *"Nation under God."* It was such an influential comment that it is even carved on the Lincoln Memorial built from 1914-17. It was not recognized as an official part of the pledge until decades later.

"In God We Trust" first appeared on the two cent piece of 1864. Congress fought for years to add a motto that best describes our nation's dependence on God. It was not until 1957 that congress first approved printing the motto on paper money. These mottos were without a doubt established ideas in the late 1800's and can be found in historical documents of the same time.

As you can see from the responses the only thing they got right was the official date of phases, when added to the pledge and paper money, not the historical truth. The reason being is that they feed off their own truths and understanding that they have developed as fact. This scenario could be acted out again with other historical truths that some non-believers choose to ignore. I do not fault them in their lack of acceptance, but only want them to know the truth. Hopefully one day some will realize that what they came to believe was propaganda aimed at tearing down Christianity. When they can come to believe they can move forward with the hope of accepting the truth.

Another good example of atheist not fully understanding history can be found in another question that was posted. The writer wanted to solicit information, and present them as facts to back up his statement.

The question was,

> *"Is it just coincidence that religious text has so much hate speech within it? Perhaps it's part of God's design to set everyone against each other with religion and then laugh at us. Your thoughts?"*

An answer given to this question perfectly demonstrates the point I was making in the previous paragraph, regarding non-believers not understanding history.

The answer that was given was,

> *Madalyn Murray O'Hair (April 13, 1919 – September 29, 1995) was an American atheist activist, and founder of the organization American Atheists and its president from 1963 to 1986. Her son, Jon Garth Murray, was the president of the organization from 1986 to 1995, while she remained de facto president during these nine years.*
>
> *She is best known for the Murray v. Curlett lawsuit, which led to a landmark Supreme Court ruling ending government sponsored prayer in American public schools. O'Hair later founded American Atheists and became so controversial that in 1964 Life magazine referred to her as "the most hated woman in America."*

In 1995 she was murdered, along with her son and granddaughter (whom she had adopted), by David Roland Waters.

It soon became clear that the writer of the answer only copy and paste paragraphs from Wikipedia.com. It is also clear the intent was to backup the claim by the writer of the question, and somehow prove that religion is violent, and full of hate. The intent was to show that a religious person was responsible for their deaths. The truth of the matter is as follows.

A murder investigation focused on David Roland Waters, who had worked as a typesetter for American Atheists. Not only did Waters have previous convictions for violent crimes, there were several suspicious burglaries during his tenure, and he pleaded guilty earlier in 1995 to stealing $54,000 from American Atheists. In the wake of the disappearance, Madalyn Murray O'Hair's estranged son William Murray publicly stated that his mother had a tendency to hire violent criminals because *"She got a sense of power out of having men in her employ who had taken human life."*

Davis Waters was tried and found guilty on the murders and was sentenced to twenty years in prison. Apparently the truth is O'Hair hired and atheist friend with a criminal past. Her death had nothing to do with any religion.

It is this deliberate attempt to present misleading information that has turned Christians into non-Christians. What most non-believers follow and believe as fact continues to be proven as lies.

Biblical Slavery

Depending on which Bible you read a common generalization is that all Christians read the scriptures for face value. This statement is true for most mundane Christians and almost every atheist. As previously discussed there are aspects of ancient Hebrew culture throughout the Old Testament, most of which are ancient Hebrew laws. Some Hebrew laws were even changed or revised in the New Testament to accommodate the changing culture and understanding of the time. One must remember the laws given in the Old Testament are only examples.

A current argument by atheists is that God allows, even approves of slavery, and for that reason He should not be followed or believed. Just like some Christians that will defend God and say that *slavery* was part of the culture and no longer applies, atheists read *slavery* as they understand by today's standards and attempt to apply that understanding to Old Testament slavery. Neither one would be right to make that assumption without properly educating themselves on ancient Hebrew laws regarding the matter.

The most popular Bible in circulation today is the KJV. It uses the word *slave* only one time, (**Jeremiah 2:14**) and the word *servant* more than five hundred times. This is an important fact when trying to understand word usage. In ancient Hebrew the word, דבע `"ebed"` means both *servant* and *slave* and the word chosen for the translation depended on usage in content. As Bible versions were happening it was common practice to interpret slavery by the standards of the time forgetting ancient Hebrew culture, as years went by the word *slave* appeared more. Take into consideration the following;

1611	KJV	the word slave appears	1 time
1882	KNJV	the word slave appears	33 times
1952	RSV	the word slave appears	83 times
1973	NIV	the word slave appears	89 times
1996	NLT	the word slave appears	102 times

The reason why the practice of slavery and servitude existed requires an understanding of ancient Hebrew culture. The main reasons for slavery and servitude are as followed; slavery to pay off a debt; slavery for a crime (when the fine could not be paid), slavery due to being poor, and slavery as prisoners of war, (the more extreme).

I will examine each and will use (*slave*) as a way to demonstrate non-believers exaggerated efforts to make the situation look worse than it was. The Hebrews made an extensive collection of laws regarding the treatment of slaves designed to protect their rights as persons.

The first I will examine is slavery due to being poor, mainly Jewish slaves.

Leviticus 25:39-40, *"And if thy brother that dwelleth by thee be waxen poor, and be sold unto thee (as a slave); thou shalt not compel him to serve as a bondservant (slave), but as a hire servant."*

43, *"Thou shalt not rule over him with regor."*

47, *"And if a sojourner or stranger wax rich by thee, and thy brother that dwelleth by him wax poor, and sell himself (as a slave)unto the stranger or sojourner by thee, or to the stock of the stranger's family."*

Deuteronomy 15:12, *"And if thy brother, a Hebrew man, or a Hebrew woman, be sold unto thee, (as a slave) and serve thee six years; then in the seventh year thou shalt let him go free from thee."*

16, *"I will not go away from thee; because he loveth thee and thine house, because he is well with thee, (slave speaking.)"*

In ancient Hebrew, to live in extreme poor meant for hard times and uncertainty. In some cases a poor person may feel better off and a better provider if he sold himself and his family into slavery rather than struggling to make it on their own. At least then he or they, would have some form of shelter, food and clothes, and be cared for. This is the reason why most scholars associate these Jews as servants rather than slaves.

Next to be reviewed is slavery for debt or crime.

Exodus 22:2-3, *"If a thief be found breaking up, and be smitten that he die, there shall be no blood be shed for him. If the sun be risen upon him, there shall be bloodshed for him, for he should make restitution; if he have nothing, then he shall be sold (as a slave in NLT) for his theft."*

Debt and crime slavery was prevalent throughout ancient Rome. A dept or crime against the government meant that one will fight as a gladiator or face being stoned to death. A debt or crime against a private citizen of Rome, (that could not be paid) meant being forced to work off such debt or crime, but only for six years.

Last is slavery as a prisoner of war, mainly non- Jewish slaves.

Deuteronomy 21:10, *"When thou goest forth to war against thine enemies, and the Lord thy God hath delivered them into hands, and thou hast taken them captive, (as slaves.)"*

Most prisoners of war that became slaves were from the neighboring Canaanites. Laws for them were not as lenient and in some cases they were slaves for the lifetime of the owner. The Jewish Bible provided religious justification for the enslavement of these neighbors. The rules governing the Canaanites were based on a curse aimed at Canaan, a son of Ham, **(Genesis 9:25-27).** In English translation of the Bible, the distinction is sometimes emphasized by translating the word "servant", "bondman", and "maidservant" in content to a Jewish slaves and using "slave" in content with non-Jewish slaves. Scholars justify the distinction because God did not want the Jews to be slaved because he freed them from Egyptian enslavement.

Leviticus 25:42, *"For they are my servants, which I brought forth out of the land of Egypt: they shall not be sold as bondmen, (slave)."*

Deuteronomy 15:15, *"And thou shalt remember that thou wast a bondman, (slave) in the land of Egypt."*

Some other Hebrew laws regarding slavery are as followed;

Exodus 20:10, *"But the seventh day is the Sabbath of the Lord thy God: in it thou shalt not do any work…, thy manservant, (slave) not thy maidservant."*

Verse 20, *"And if a man smite his servant, (slave) or his maid, with a rod, and he died under his hand; he shall be surely punished."*

Verse 26-27, *"And if a man smite the eye of his servant, (slave) or the eye of his maid, that it perish; he shall let him go free for his eye's sake. And if he smite out his manservant's, (slave) tooth, or his maidservant's took; he shall let him go free for his tooth's sake."*

Exodus 23:9, *"Thou shalt not oppress a stranger, (slave)… seeing ye were strangers, (slaves) in the land of Egypt."*

Verse 12, *"Six days thou shalt do thy work, and on the seventh day thou shalt rest… and the son of thy handmaid, and the stranger, (slave), may be refreshed."*

Deuteronomy 23:15-16, *"Thou shalt not deliver unto his master the servant (slave) which is escaped from his master unto thee: He shall dwell with thee, even among you, in that place which he shall choose in one of thy gates, where it liketh him best: thou shalt not oppress him."*

Deuteronomy 24; 7, *"If a man be found stealing any of his brother of the children of Israel, and maketh merchandise, (slave) of him, or selleth him; then that thief shall die."*

Verse 14, *"Thou shall not oppress an hired servant, (slave) that is poor and needy, whether he be thy brother or thy strangers."*

At the end of his six years of service, by Hebrew law, he was set free under his own accord. Not just that but under Hebrew law he was required to be provided with cattle and grain for his service. This is not how slaves were treated in previous times as we know.

Exodus 21:2-3, *"If thou buy an Hebrew servant, (slave), six years he shall serve: and in the seventh he shall go out free. If he came in by himself, he shall go out by himself: if he were married, then his wife shall go out with him."*

Leviticus 25:40-41, *"But as an hired servant, (slave) and as a sojourner, he shall be with thee, and shall serve thee unto the year of jubilee: And then shall he depart from thee, both he and his children with him, and shall return unto his family."*

Deuteronomy 15:12-14, *"And if thy brother, an Hebrew man, or an Hebrew woman, be sold unto thee (as a slave), and serve thee six years; then in the seventh year thou shalt let him go free from thee. And when thou sendest him out free, thou shalt not let him go away empty: Thou shalt furnish him liberally out of thy flock, and out of thy floor, and out of thy winepress: of that wherewith the Lord thy God hath blessed thee yhou shalt give upon him."*

These laws were to be obeyed by all servant owners and applied to all servants. In the eyes of God all servants were equal and therefore must be treated as equal.

Leviticus 24:22, *"Ye shall have one manner of law, as well for the stranger (slave), as for one of your own country: for I am the Lord your God."*

There exists biblical evidence that suggests that not the entire Hebrew slave laws were followed as originally intended. God defends his intention and reminds the Hebrews of his covenant.

Jeremiah 34:13-16, *"Thus saith the Lord, the God of Israel; I made a covenant with your fathers in the day that I brought them forth out of the land of Egypt, out of the house of bondman, saying, At the end of seven years let ye go every man his brother an Hebrew, which hath been sold unto thee; and when he hath served thee six years, thou shalt let him go free from thee: but your fathers hearkened not unto me, neither inclined their ears. And ye were now turned, and had done right in my sight, in proclaiming liberty every man to his neighbor; and ye had made a covenant before me in the house which is called by my name: But ye turned and polluted my name, and caused every man his servant, and every man his handmaid, whom he had set at liberty at their pleasure, to return, and brought them into subjection, to be unto you for servants and for handmaids."*

In conclusion on the topics of slavery, it is to be clearly understood that biblical slavery was in no comparison to the slavery we understand in the twenty first century. Considering both the reason and term of servitude there is no logical reason to compare the two, or believe that servitude was an unmoral act within the Bible

Product of Free Will

Many Christians believe God gave all humans free will. That we were given the freedom to decide for ourselves what to do with our life, and what form of faith we practice. Free will is the purported ability of people to make choices free from constraints. The principle of free will has religious and ethical implications. For example, in the religious realm, free will implies that an omnipotent divinity does not assert its power over individual will and choices. In ethics, it may hold implications regarding whether individuals can be held morally accountable for their actions. The question of free will has been a central issue since the beginning of philosophical thought. The problem of free will assumed quite a new character with the advent of the Christian religion. The doctrine that developed is that God created man, has commanded him to obey the moral law, and has promised to reward or punish him for observance or violation of this law. Unless man is really free, he cannot be justly held responsible for his actions.

Take everyday decisions for example. You wake up and make the decision on what to wear. You decide what to eat. If you have more than one car you decide which one to drive. Which way do you go to work, how fast to drive. You make decision on what to eat, where do you eat it. You decide on how productive you are going to be and if you will work late or not. Then when you get home, you decide what is for dinner, what you watch and how late do you stay up. Every decision no matter how small has consequence latter. *Free will* implies that we make our decision without implication and have to accept the outcome, without blaming someone else. Rather it is Biblically sound or an everyday fact *free will* does exists.

Remember the story of Adam and Eve in the Bible? The chapter in Genesis perfectly describes the origin of *free will* and the consequence of the decision to disobey God. We are the living results of the decisions made by our father and fore-fathers. The Bible reads in **John 8:38,**

"And ye do that which ye have seen with your father,"

Verse 41, *"Ye do the deeds of your father."*

This world exists today, in its current state, because of those early decisions. Free will, although a great gift, has negative impacts when used to make careless and thoughtless decisions based on irrational ideas.

As humans *we* are responsible for the world's current state, not God. Blaming God is our way of not accepting responsibility for our actions. We cannot blame God or organized religion for the problems that plague today's culture and society, not just here but worldwide. Mankind created our issues, so it is up to us to solve them, if we can only ask God for guidance.

For atheists who are lost in faith, trust and love are not easily received. Being full of doubt and hesitant to trust new things leaves most atheists closed to new ideas. Most atheists are convinced that they are truly free to live their life as they see fit. They are not tied down to anything, nor owe tithings to any religion. They feel that they can say and do whatever they want without worrying about committing sins or their own morality. For them it is much easier and more satisfying to reject God than to understand His reasons. Most people fear what they do not understand. It is human nature to want to see proof in order to believe. It is said in the Bible that you must accept God as your Savior and be born again if you want to go to Heaven.

Romans 10:13, *"For whosoever shall call upon the name of the Lord shall be saved,"*

John 3:3, *"Jesus answered and said unto him, Verily, verily, I say unto thee, except a man be born again, he cannot see the kingdom of God."*

John 3:15, *"That whosoever believeth in him should not perish, but have eternal life."*

Unless atheists change their beliefs they will be doomed to eternity in the Christian hell. It will take much more than waiting until their death bed to accept Jesus out of fear. Atheists, although living free in this life on earth will be forever slaves to torment in the believed afterlife of Christians. We can only pray for the blind to see and the helpless to help themselves, for change can only take place in the hearts of the needy and weak.

What I personally find most interesting about atheists is their uncanny knowledge of the Holy Bible. They are well-informed of the verses of the Bible, but like previously mention they lack a poor understanding of the content they are reading. They fail to understand why and to whom the books were written. They spend so much time reading, studying, and trying to pick it apart that they are forgetting the most important fact. The Bible is a collection of historical writings;

contained within it are the events and culture practices of a society that lived more than two thousand years ago. I once compared atheists to holy rollers, (people who take the Bible literally) because like holy rollers atheists believe they are reading the alleged words of God. They believe everything contained within supposedly happened exactly the way it reads with no room for interpretation. They fail to understand the concept of metaphors and parables, and how they relate to Jesus' teaching. Their biggest fault regarding the Bible is taking the context as a current message that should be applied to everyone in today's culture and society. They fail to understand and except the fact that the Bible was written for the culture and people of two thousand years ago. The Bible's authors wrote about events they saw, and the problems they were facing. They documented the everyday struggles they were facing as a new religion. Events like crucifixion, slavery, the treatment of women and stoning someone to death do not apply in today's society.

1 Corinthians 14:34-35

Some non-believers criticize the Bible fare treatment of women because they read this scripture as literal. Even some Christian sects have interpreted this verse as women not being allowed to preach the word of God. When a Southern Baptist Minster met with me to discuss this book, he laugh and criticized my church for having a female preacher. His own words were,

"I see she doesn't follow the words of the Lord."

Atheists and others feel that a book that discriminates should not be used as religious guidance and morality, another reason why not to believe in God. Some male ministers will even argue that God forbids females from preaching the word of God and should not speak in church.

1 Corinthians 14:34-35, *"Let your women keep silence in the churches: for it is not permitted unto them to speak: but they are commanded to be*

under obedience, as also saith the law. And if they will learn anything, let them ask their husbands at home: for it is a shame for women to speak in the church."

Paul stayed over a year and a half in Corinth, **(Acts 18:11)**, around 51-53 A.D. Corinth's population consisted of Jews, Gentiles ex-Roman soldiers and heathens. When St. Paul wrote to the Corinthians he was addressing the issues that plagued their society and their church. The city of Corinth was famous for its debauchery and cult prostitutes. The Greeks had a proverb about the city which tells a great deal about its moral decay, *"It is not every man who can afford a journey to Corinth."*

Those who were worldly wise used the verb *"corinthianize"* to describe an act of immorality. Paul was informed of a case of gross immorality in the church, one with which the church had not dealt with. Instead of feeling shame and sorrow over this sin, at least some of the church leaders were proud of their tolerance.

1 Corinthians 5:1, *"It is reported commonly that there is fornication among you."*

The church received little respect as a church of God. Women were gossiping during church and talking out. They had little respect for their husbands, and the city was struggling between heathenism and Christianity. Paul also received information of unbecoming conduct of church members at the Lord's Supper. Church members were over indulging in both wine and bread.

1 Corinthians 11:27-29, *"Wherefore whosoever shall eat this bread, and drink this cup of the Lord, unworthily, shall be guilty of the body and blood of the Lord. But let a man examine himself, and so let him eat of that bread, and drink of that cup. For he that eateth and drinketh unworthily, eateth and drinketh damnation to himself, not discerning the Lord's body."*

The church of Corinth was corrupt, and failed to properly educate the congregation on the message of Jesus. The letter was meant as a plea for the church to *"get it together."*

Rape in the Bible
Another Bible story that atheists use as an argument is **Deuteronomy 22:28-29** which reads,

"If a man finds a damsel that is a virgin, which is not betrothed, and lay hold on her, and lie with her, and they be found; Then the man that lay with her shall give unto the damsel's father fifty shekels of silver, and she shall be his wife."

Atheists claim that God supports rape in the Bible based on translation from NIV and NLT. I have seen atheists recite the verse, and claim it to be from the New Living Translation, (NLT). The atheists quote, *"If a man is caught in the act of raping a young woman who is not engaged, he must pay fifty pieces of silver to her father."* Rape is used in this translation. The reason atheists use both the NIV and NLT translation in their arguments, is because they are the only two Bibles that have the word, *"rape"* within their verses. The translators of those Bibles claim to get their sources from the best possible Hebrew and Greek texts. Let us evaluate their accuracy. In their translation they replaced *and lay on her, and lie with her* with one word *rape*. Is rape used in the original text? The answer is no. There is no corresponding Hebrew or Greek word for *rape*. The Greek word used for *and lay on* is μεμνήστευται in Hebrew it is שפת pronounce as *taphas* both mean *to handle, lay hold and take hold*. The Greek word for *and lie with* is βιασάμενος in Hebrew it is בכש pronounced as *shakab* means *to lie down*. The act in question could simple be a situation in which an unengaged virgin was caught having sex, or being alone with a man without a chaperone. In either case the women would have been consider unclean and unmarriageable. Considering at that time that a women's fate depended on her ability to get married a father would force the man to marry her, this is in accordance with Hebrew Law. In the time of ancient Israel men insisted their brides to be virgins, they had the right to seek prove of her virginity. If there was no blood on the marital sheets she faces the possibility of being stoned to death. All other Bible versions read the original text as intended. The NIV and NLT translators interpret the verse as the women being *rape* of her future. If atheists want to claim the act of rape in the Bible they would read verse 25. **Verse 25,**

"But if a man finds a betrothed damsel in the field, and the man force her, and lie with her: then the man only that lay with her shall die."

The verse is a clear indication that forcible rape held a death penalty in the Bible. Clearly the atheists will not use a verse that shows God's disapproval of rape and proof of the consequences of the sin. Using an obvious verse would destroy an atheist's argument so they have to pick and chose which Bibles to quote from.

Non-believers claim that God supports the stoning to death of sinners, because it is in the Bible.

John 8:7, *"He that is without sin among you, let him cast a stone at her."*

In the story Jesus does not say to stone the woman, even after she sinned. Stoning to death an individual was meant for serious crimes, law breaker and even for those who disgrace their family. It was consider instant justice, like a mob mentality. It was an unfortunate part of ancient Israel; an event that played out in the public's eye, witness and recorded by many. Atheists tend to misunderstand the meaning of the stories. They think one-sided wanting only to disprove the Bible. They fail to embrace and understand the history that developed into the making of Christianity, and the message behind the scriptures. Just because they read it in the Bible, it does not mean that those are the words of God, nor actions approved by God they were simply words written by man expressing what they understood and seen.

A study showed that most students lose their faith around the second year of college. They have to devote more time to school, studying, working, and outside influences such as partying, dating, internet, FaceBook updates, texting, and watching HDTV. The majority of students lives on campus and therefore is less likely to go to church on Sundays. They have to deal with peer pressure; therefore they are less likely to be open about their faith due to their overwhelming need to feel accepted by fellow students and fear of belittlement for their religious views. After numerous years in college it becomes much harder to regain their faith. What was learned in college was to make you think logically and rationally, both of which contradict religion which is primarily based on faith.

My niece came down to visit me during her two week winter break from college. While talking she mention to me that a friend showed her a YouTube video about Christianity. This is a common video that falsely compares Jesus to pagan Gods. Her friend told her while watching the video, *"This is why I have my views on religion."* I explained to my niece that all the supposed evidence of connections was falsely based and some were just straight forward lies. I spent the next hour listing the correct information and explained how they made the false connections and the motive for doing so.

What do you do if you lost your faith, or just never new Jesus because of lack of involvement? The first step to believing in God is accepting the possibility of the existence of Jesus Christ as He was portrayed in the Bible. It is easy to believe that Jesus lived a moral and ethical life. The same way of living we should be emulating today as Christians. Many different religious groups accept the existence of Jesus, but not as the son of God. More like a great prophet or an enlightened teacher who was very close to God. Once you accept Him, study His known life and what He did with His disciples. You will understand what it means to be like Jesus and how we should strive to live a moral life. Everyone, no matter Christian or other faith would benefit from living this moral and ethical life. As followers of Christ it is our responsibility to try to achieve perfect harmony with each other while living on this planet.

All Christians are not the same

Christianity is completely misunderstood and in some cases practiced wrong by its own followers. Christianity itself is a single word with a broad meaning. It cannot be easily defined because of the vast differences that the one hundred and forty plus divisions represent. Atheists see Christianity as Christianity and Christians as Christians, as if we are all alike in manner of thought, worship and belief. This misconception I called the *"Christianity blanket."* No matter what division of Christianity you belong to or how deep your faith is you remain under this *"Christianity blanket."* It does not matter what we believe as individuals or how true to Christianity we are, we are all looked at by atheists as *"Christians."* We and other faiths then become the reason for all of the world's problems. With so many divisions and so many diverse practices, a person can range from mildly Christian to *the "extreme Christian."* The fact remains that Christians are heavily disliked by atheists, Muslims, and some Jewish segments. The only way to change this view is to unite the divisions under Jesus Christ as one church. All the church leaders from the more than one hundred and forty plus divisions need to come together and agree to change Christianity back to Christianity. Focus Christianity on the basics of the faith and on what Jesus taught us. Until this unity occurs we will always be targets for the non believers. Christians and organized religion will continue to be blamed for the world's problems and perceived as untrue Christians. With the current state of our society, the chance of a union is slim to none. All divisions need to rethink the meaning of Christianity and look deeply inside themselves to see if what they are preaching is what Jesus intended for us to follow. The fate of Christianity will rest in the hands of our future generations. We must properly educate them on what it means to be Christians and how to forever preserve the teachings of Jesus. Unless we take drastic actions to correct the perception of Christianity, it just might end up a lost religion and a meaningless faith.

I personally believe that God has a divine plan for everyone. That is, everyone is here for a reason. Your life has been carefully structured to lead you into the direction of faith. When you get off track God intervenes. He cannot stop free will, but He can redirect your life with events. Therefore I believe everything happens for a reason. The reason may not reveal itself for some time. Patience and faith are both crucial when trying to understand God's plan.

A personal life event

I was seventeen, hunting with a friend in the woods behind his house. We spent hours scouting with no luck. On the way home we decided to shoot at some targets in a field. He fired one shot. The bullet ricocheted off a tree hitting me above my left knee. The bullet fragment chipped my kneecap, tore ligaments in my knee, and then traveled down my femur. I could not walk for a week. I limped around school like I was crippled. A year later I enrolled in the United States Army hoping to follow in my father's footsteps. I had my life planned out for the next eight years. I was going to spend the next four years in the military. When released I would use the G.I. Bill to pay for the next four years of college. One day I met with the Army recruiter for one of our planned monthly meetings. I was on the delayed entry program: I was already in the Army, but I had to wait until I graduated to leave for boot camp. While going over some early training details he noticed I was limping. Since the accident, my knee occasionally swelled up and my joints would get stiff, preventing me from walking without an awkward limp. He asked me if I was okay; it was at that time that I informed him of what had happened the previous year. It was his duty to report it to be sure I was fit enough to continue with my military career. He had me meet Army medical doctors who in turn requested that I see a specialist. The testing revealed damaged tissue and ligaments. Since my knee was still swollen, the doctors had concerns with my knee's ability to handle the intense training the new recruits would be subjected to on a daily basis. He reported his findings to the Army. Only one month before I was scheduled to leave for boot camp, I received a letter in the mail. The letter was a medical discharge document ending my ability to join because of the damage to my knee. I remembered thinking to myself *what am I going to do.* All my plans were based on a military career. All of my friends were going to college, and I was going nowhere. I had no backup plans. I had never considered college as an option. This was another turning point in my life. My life would not be what it is today if not for that accident. There is no way that my life, as I know it, would be the way it is nor could I have the things I have. I love my beautiful wife and the three great kids she blessed me with. My family has increased five times over. I would not trade any of my life's events, nor do I wish things were different. If any small events either good or bad would not have happened, it would not have led to what my life is today. This is why I believe in God's plan.

Chapter 5:
Why? Why? Why?

"Love never says it owns something, though it owns everything. Love does not say, "This is mine" or "That is mine," but rather, "All that is mine is yours."
The Gospel of Philip

Everything we were taught about Christianity was learned from both the Holy Bible and church leaders. As practicing Christians you may never have thought twice about some common events and stories that we know and practice. There are stories about holidays that are not mentioned in the Bible. There are phrases that we say and believe, and dates that we cherish as Christians that are notably absent from the Bible as well. Where did they come from? Why do we cherish them? How do we know that Jesus was born on December twenty fifth? Why do we call it Good Friday, and what was good about Jesus dying on the cross? Why do we call it Easter and what does Easter mean? Where did the concept of the Trinity come from since it is not in the Bible? How many Christians do you know that blindly follow tradition without ever asking why? As a follower of Christ I believe it to be very important to understand our early history and why we do the things we do. Understanding such complex ideas will strengthen your belief in Jesus and give you an understanding of how our religion was formed into what we have today.

The History of Christmas (Traditional Thinking)

As Christianity was struggling for acceptance, they had to include festivals that appealed to the pagans that wanted something more. There were hundreds of thousands of pagans in the known world, all of which had a vested interest in the survival of their belief and way of life. The first recorded step to make Christianity appealing to the pagans was to use dates of pagan celebrations for Christian celebrations. Some people will claim that Christians copied December twenty fifth, which was already use by the Romans to celebrate the Natalis Solic Invicti, *(Birth of the Unconquered Son)*. It was also believed to be the birthday of Mithras, the Romans version of Mithra the Persian Sun God who also became known as *"the Sun of Righteousness."* He was a favorite pagan god among the Roman soldiers and slaves. The religion of Mithra predates Christianity by over six hundred years, but was only practiced in Persia before migrating to Rome around the first and second centuries. It is important to mention that very little historical evidence exists to support any claims regarding Mithra. Most of the information acquired about Mithras comes from excavation of early Mithraic temples and early writings from Christians such as Justin Martyr. Modern accounts rely primarily on modern interpretation of reliefs.

The date of the Solic Invicti fell toward the end of the Roman winter celebration called Saturnalia. The Saturnalia was a week long winter celebration from December seventeenth to the twenty-third. The colder weather meant less farm work which, in turn, made for a great time to celebrate the season. Christians wanted to introduce Pagans to Christianity by using December twenty fifth as another reason to celebrate, *"the birth of Jesus Christ."* It was believed that converting would be easier. This has been accepted by traditional thinking, and among those who chose to ignore the full history.

Historical Facts on Christmas

Historical dates and time lines proves that early Christians did not copy December twenty fifth from pagan festivals. In 221 A.D. Sextus Julius Africanus, a Christian historian and traveler known as *"Father of Christian Chronography"*, first popularized December twenty fifth as Jesus' birthday. Julius believed the world was created on March twenty-fifth, (vernal equinox). Just like creation the vernal equinox represented the beginning of life. It was also the first day of the medieval Julian calendar. It is important to mention that when the Julian calendar was originally designed the vernal equinox actually fell on March twenty-fifth. Julius also believed that Christ was conceived, what we now call the *Annunciation,* on March twenty-fifth. According to Julius since the word of God was incarnate on March twenty-fifth, Jesus would be born nine months later on December twenty-fifth. This thinking came from the old Jewish idea of the "*integral age,*" that great prophets were conceived on the same day as their death. Like so many orthodox Christians Julius believed life starts at conception.

There were some proofs presented to support the Annunciation in March. The first established that the division of Abijah overlapped the Feast of Tabernacles, October 3-10, 6 B.C. With the conception of John the Baptist on October tenth, the Annunciation fell about five and a half months later, or on March 25, 5 B.C.

Second, Luke records the Annunciation in the sixth month, which is interpreted to mean the sixth calendar month of the year. According to Luke's Syro-Macedonian reckoning this lunar month fell from March 10 to April 7, 5 B.C.

Hippolytus of Rome (170-236 A.D.), also an early church writer mentions in one of his best manuscripts December twenty-fifth as a possible date of the birth of Jesus. As we find in his **Commentary to Daniel 4.23.3** he writes.

> *"For the first advent of our Lord in the flesh, when he was born in Bethlehem, eight days before the kalends of January (December twenty fifth), the 4th day of the week (Wednesday), while Augustus was in his forty-second year."*

Fifty years later in 274 A.D. the Emperor Aurelian (214-275 A.D.) designated December twenty fifth as the festival of *Sol Invictus,* (winter solstice), which the Romans referred to as Bruma. Emperor Aurelian was the second of several successful "*soldier-emperors.*" The coins of his time show that Aurelian promoted his army. He celebrated their unity, loyalty, and bravery. At this time there was fierce religious competition with the growing Christian faith. Aurelian wanted to strengthen the position of the *Sun God* as the main divinity of the Roman pantheon. He wanted to ensure the soldiers pagan religion of Mithras would continue. This is why he was the first to make December twenty-fifth an official civil holiday, proclaiming it to be the birthday of Mithras and the date of the *Sol Invictus*. It is important to mention that December twenty-fifth held no specific festival date to pagans. As mention before the Saturnalia winter festival ended on Dec. twenty-third. Before this time, the winter solstice, *Sol Invictus*, was December twenty- first. The earliest known date of the Sol Invictus as a winter festival, not associated with Mithras, was is in a dedication for Rome in 158 A.D. The above event happed well after early Christians developed the idea of Jesus' birthday. This is proof; once and for all, that early Christians were the first to use December twenty-fifth, but it was not an "official" holiday until later.

It was the Western Christians who were the first to officially celebrate Christmas as early as 336 A.D., after Constantine legalized Christian worship. In 350 A.D., December twenty fifth was added to the Roman calendar as a feast day. It wasn't until 440 A.D., that the Orthodox Church officially proclaimed that December twenty fifth was the birthday of our Lord Jesus Christ. The rest of the story is Christian history.

The fact remains that Christians were in the Roman Empire before the religion of Mithras migrated over around the first and second centuries, Jesus' birthday on December twenty-fifth was already an idea fifty years before the date of the Sol Invictus was chosen, and used to establish the birthday of Mithras. It is unfair to accuse early Christians from borrowing anything from the religion of Mithras. It is in fact the Persian Mithra that is believed to have influence Christianity, because it predates the Roman's Mithras. Historical evidence shows no real comparison between the two. In fact Christianity has more perceived similarities with the Roman Mithras. Why is this? The religion of

Mithras slightly changed in both belief and practices to fit the Roman idea of the deity as it migrated over mingling with Christians. It is more likely that the Roman Mithras borrowed ideas from Christianity than vice versa.

The idea of a relationship between early Christianity and Mithraism is based on a remark in the second century Christian writer Justin Martyr, who accused the Mithraists of diabolically imitating the Christian communion rite.

> *"For the apostles, in the memoirs composed by them, which are called Gospels, have thus delivered unto us what was enjoined upon them; that Jesus took bread, and when He had given thanks, said, "This do ye in remembrance of Me, this is My body; "and that, after the same manner, having taken the cup and given thanks, He said, "This is My blood; "and gave it to them alone. Which the wicked devils have imitated in the mysteries of Mithras, commanding the same thing to be done. For, that bread and a cup of water are placed with certain incantations in the mystic rites of one who is being initiated; you either know or can learn."*
> **Justin Martyr,** First Apology, **Ch. 66**

Why do so many non-believers claim that Christians copied from Pagans? There are some traditions that were carried over to Christianity by pagan converts. When pagans converted they brought with them their families customs and traditions. The *Twelve Days of Christmas* originated from Northern Europe, who was the last to be Christianized. There, it was the twelve day pre-Christmas winter festival known as *Christmas Jule.* The *"Yule Log"* comes from the lighting of logs to honor Thor, an ancient pagan god from Germanic mythology. It was popular to decorate trees, and later came caroling, dancing, and gift giving. Early Christians started to incorporate the story of Jesus' birth into the festival giving way to what we all know today as Christmas.

Jesus was born earlier

Was the date of His birth right? Evidence suggests that His birth date was months earlier than December. It is believed that when Jesus died on March of 30 A.D., he was thirty three and a half years old. In order for the months to add up correctly, you have to count six months onward from March. When you do so, you get the September/October time frame. Also biblical evidence tells us that the shepherds were watching their flocks in the fields.

Luke 2:8, *"And there were in the same country shepherds abiding in the field, keeping watch over their flocks by night."*

Jerusalem is a very cold place in the winter; it snows there every year starting as early as November. They experience a major snow event of more than one foot once in every seven years. The shepherds would have had a hard time finding grass for their flock once it was covered with snow, and the cold temperatures would have been too much for both the flocks and the shepherds. Shepherds are only in their fields from March through October, when the weather is warm enough to support the growth of grass. These simple facts do imply a different date.

Is the date right

Does it matter? The important thing is that we celebrate His birth, and what better time of year than a winter festival. It becomes clear why Christians used December twenty fifth once you understand the history and the reasons. Because of that date many more pagans would flock to convert to Christianity, and soon the religion would dominate the known world. Many Christians acknowledge that no one knows the exact day Jesus was born. The precise date of Jesus' birth is not critical and will always be argued, therefore speculation and controversy about this topic will cause Christians to lose focus of the point.

It is important that we rejoice and celebrate the central events in the life of Jesus Christ because he is the core and foundation of our faith.

When we think about and ponder his birth, there are many issues that are mysterious and profound for us. God came to us, taking human flesh, dwelling with us, so that we might be saved. He never stopped being God, but he also became human. He was born of a virgin, and began his human life as a helpless and dependent baby, just as we all do.

To Celebrate, or not to Celebrate

The question remains, did Jesus intend for us to celebrate His birthday? It is never mentioned in the Bible if He celebrated His birthday or any other known writing of the time. There is nothing explicit in the Bible that commands us to celebrate or not to celebrate birthdays. Rather, the Bible has given us a general guide on this issue when it says that we should each be convinced in our *own* minds as to the importance or non-importance of a particular day, and that it should be a matter for the conscience of the individual, between them and God, as to whether we celebrate that day or not.

Romans 14:5, *"One indeed judges a day above another day; and another one judges every day alike. Let each one be fully assured in his own mind. The one minding the day, he minds it to the Lord. And the one not minding the day, he does not mind it to the Lord. The one eating, he eats to the Lord; for he gives thanks to God. And the one not eating, he does not eat to the Lord, and gives thanks to God."*

Even with this scripture in mind His birthday was never celebrated for the first two hundred years. Early church leaders even argued that it would be wrong to celebrate His birth. Only pagan gods were honored with birthdays, not the son of God born free of sins. The first century Jewish historian Josephus noted that Jewish families did not celebrate birthdays:

> *"Nay, indeed, the law does not permit us to make festivals at the birth of our children, and thereby afford occasion of drinking to excess."* **(Josephus. Translated by W.**

Whiston. Against Apion, **Book II, Chapter 26. From Josephus Complete Works, Kregel Publications, Grand Rapids (MI), 14th printing, 1977, p. 632).**

In 245 A.D. in response to the floating idea of Jesus' birthday the early church historian Origen argued,

"...of all the holy people in the Scriptures, no one is recorded to have kept a feast or held a great banquet on his birthday. It is only sinners (like Pharaoh and Herod) who make great rejoicings over the day on which they were born into this world below." **(Origen, in Levit., Hom. VIII, in Migne P.G., XII, 495)**

The ultimate decision to celebrate His birth was based on the nature of His life. He was born a man and lived a moral life. Modern day Christians with the exception of Jehovah's Witnesses acknowledges their own birth so it only makes since it seems to acknowledge His too.

Jehovah's Witnesses often reject birthdays as "pagan" and will therefore refuse to participate in them. In addition to this, Witnesses also reject birthdays because they claim that they are placed in an unfavorable light in the Bible.

In regard to the notion that birthdays being of pagan origin, a Watchtower publication states the following.

"Le livres des religions (The Book of Religions), an encyclopedia widely distributed in France, calls this custom a ritual and lists it among "secular rites." Although considered to be a harmless secular custom day, birthday celebrations are actually rooter in paganism. The Encyclopedia Americana (1991 edition) states: The ancient world of Egypt, Greece, Rome, and Persia celebrated the birthdays of gods, kings, and nobles." **(Jehovah's Witnesses and Education, p. 15.)**

Another publication says,

> *"Do Bible references to birthday celebrations put them in a favorable light? The Bible makes only two references to such celebrations...Jehovah's Witnesses take note that God's Word reports unfavorably about birthday celebrations and to shun these."* **(Reasoning from the Scriptures, pp. 68-69).**

In the Bible there are some stories with references to a birthday celebration, all of which have negative results. In Matthew, John the Baptist is beheaded as a birthday gift to his daughter, instructed by her mother.

Matthew 14:10, *"And he sent, and beheaded John in the prison."*

In the book of Job **(Chapter 1:4-19)** all ten of his children are killed by Satan during his birthday celebration. Some other Bible authors write about their dislike of birthdays.

Job 3:3, *"Let the day perish wherein I was born, and the night in which it was said, There is a man child conceived."*

Genesis 40:20-21, *"And it came to pass the third day, which was Pharaoh's birthday, that he made a feast unto all his servants: and he lifted up the head of his chief butler and of the chief baker among his servants."*

Ecclesiastes 7:1, *"A good name is better than precious ointment; and the day of death than the day of one's birth."*

Jeremiah 20:14, *"Cursed be the day wherein I was born: let not the day wherein my mother bare me be blessed."*

Did the Bible authors know something we did not? Since we are born in sin, is our birth into a sinful world worth celebrating? Are we celebrating His birth for our own selfish needs? We should celebrate what it means to be Followers of Christ, because His birth was the dawn of a new age.

Forgetting Jesus
Did our society get so caught up in the Christmas season that we actually replaced Jesus' birth with Santa Claus and trees? The holiday season brings forth billions of dollars annually selling trees, ornaments, lights, figurines, wrapping paper, gifts and Santa, most of which have pagan origins. When you go shopping you see all of this with little or no Jesus. Why did we forget the meaning? You can ask young children the meaning of Christmas and you will hear answers such as Santa, trees and gifts. Unless we educate our children and bring Jesus back into the Christmas holiday, the true meaning of the celebration will be buried and forgotten.

The History of Easter
The most important and oldest Christian holiday beside the Sabbath is Easter Sunday. It is by far the holiest of all Christian celebrations. Easter marks the beginning of the spring season during the vernal equinox, (March 21), when the day and night have equal share. The beginning of spring represents the resurrection of nature from a long dormant winter, bringing forth new life for a new beginning.

Why is it important for Christians to celebrate the Easter Season? Jesus was crucified on Good Friday to save us from our sins, and His resurrection from death after three days is the foundation of the Christian faith. The season owes it roots deep into the book of Exodus. The annual Jewish festival, the Passover or Pesach, commemorates the Israelites' exodus from Egypt after three hundred years of slavery and bondage. Although the Passover was already established and has been practiced for hundreds of years, it was about to take on another means of celebration. It started on Palm Sunday when Jesus road into Jerusalem on a donkey to celebrate the Feast of Passover and Unleavened Bread. His arrival was adorned by Jews laying down palm leaves for Him to ride in on. It was a welcome fit for a king. After all He was from the blood line of King David. The Jews perceived Him as the *"Messiah King"* mentioned in the Old Testament which said that He would free them.

Jeremiah 23:5-6, *"Behold, the days come, saith the Lord, that I will raise unto David a righteous Branch, and a King shall reign and prosper, and shall execute judgement and justice in the earth. In his days Judah shall be saved, and Israel shall dwell safely: and this is his name whereby he shall be called, THE LORD OUR RIGHTEOUSNESS."*

In **Zechariah 6:12-13,** *"And speak unto him, saying, thus speaketh the Lord of hosts, saying, behold the man whose name is The Branch: and he shall grow up out of his place, and he shall build the temple of the Lord. Even he shall build the temple of the Lord; and he shall bear the glory, and shall sit and rule upon his throne; and he shall be a priest upon his throne: and the counsel of peace shall be between them both."*

The Jews have been worked up for hundreds of years waiting for a king to free them. These same Jews would eventually turn against Him because Jesus did not fit the image of a mighty king. For His crimes of blasphemy and claiming to be the *"King of the Jews,"* the head priest, Caiaphas, **(John 18:13-28)** and the Jews wanted Him punished. Under orders from Pontius Pilate He was crucified. He endured a slow and painful death, which He already knew was coming. He warned His disciples at the Last Supper that he would be betrayed and to, *"Do this in memory of me,"* referring to receiving the body and blood of Christ or Eucharist. On Good Friday, Jesus died. The exact date of His death varies depending on the source. The theologian Tertullian gives us March 25, 29 A.D. Other sources claim as late as April 3, 33 A.D.

What was good about His death? His death on the cross symbolized freeing us from our sins, eventually saving us. God's only son Jesus gave up His life for all of humanity.

John 3:16, *"For God so loved the world that he gave his only begotten Son, that whosoever believeth in him should not perish, but have everlasting life."*

It is the first documented act of heroism, one person giving his life so another can live. Three days later Jesus rose from the dead as He foretold in the scriptures. Resurrection Sunday reminds us of the promise Jesus made about salvation, and the promise of life after death in The Kingdom of Heaven. These stories were foretold by the prophets of the Old Testament further establishing Jesus' divinity as the son of God.

Why do we call it Easter? The word Easter is used to match the name of an old spring celebration used by pagans. Like Christmas, it was believed to be easier for pagans to better accept Christianity. Some current traditions that are derived from early pagan influences were the hare and eggs. The hare and the eggs represent fertility, and the colors of eggs represent the colors brought forth by spring. These are ancient pagan fertility rituals that still endure today. The Easter celebration was well established by the second century. The exact date changes year from year. Eventually it was decided that Easter would follow the first full moon after the vernal equinox. Therefore Easter would always be celebrated around March 21- April 25, as decided by Constantine during the Council of Nicaea in 325 A.D. By the fourth century Good Friday had become a separate holiday to Easter Sunday, or Resurrection Sunday. The modern English term, Easter, comes from the old English word for Eostre, or Eoaster, (The Goddess of Fertility.) It refers to Eostur-Monath a month in the Germanic calendar. Named after the goddess of Anglo-Saxon paganism and knowing the Germanic calendar, we know that Eostur-Monath equals the month of April. Eostur-Monath eventually died out and was replaced by the Christian Easter Celebration around the second century.

Why is Easter not mentioned in the Bible? Actually it is. The word Easter can be found in **Acts 12:4** in the KJV,

"And when he had apprehended him, he put him in prison, and delivered him to four quaternion's of soldiers to keep him; intending after Easter to bring him forth to the people."

The word Easter is used incorrectly and can only be found in both the KJV and 21st.CKJV. Since Easter was already practiced, King James' scholars inadvertently used Easter in place of Pesach, the Passover. The word error is widely known in the biblical world, and it is a further example of how word usage changes over time with Bible versions. But again, were we meant to observe Easter Sunday. Is it even appropriate to honor Jesus' death? As Christians we recognize one event from that Passover weekly. During every church service most Christians participate in the eating of bread and drinking of wine in memory of Jesus. He asked us during the last supper to remember Him.

In **Acts 2:42,** *"And they continued stedfastly in the apostle's doctrine and fellowship, and in breaking of bread, and in prayers."*

We know from the time Luke wrote Acts they were remembering Him as early as 62 A.D. In Paul epistle to the Colossians, he reminds their church that Jesus is first and foremost in everything we do and must be remembered. He foresees the future of Christianity and knows what will become of Christians holidays.

Colossians 2:16-17, *"Let no man therefore judge you in meat, or in drink, or in respect of an holyday, or of the new moon, or of the Sabbath days: which are a shadow of things to come."*

With so many biblical references to worship all Christians should have a collective understanding on God's desire, yet some Christians do not worship Easter and would argue that we should not because of its pagan roots. They use Bible scriptures as their defense.

Jeremiah 10:2, *"Thus saith the Lord, learn not the way of the heathen."*

Deuteronomy 12:30-32, *"Take heed to thyself that thou be not snared by following them, after that they be destroyed from before thee; and that thou enquire not after their gods, saying, How did these nations serve their gods? Even so will I do likewise. Thou shalt not do so unto the Lord thy God; for every abomination to the Lord, which he hateth, have they done unto their gods; for even their sons and their daughters they have burnt in the fire to their gods."*

If one follows the Bible literally, they will not want to participate in rituals with pagan roots as not to offend God.

Holidays have become so socialized that manufactures and businesses have found it more profitable to appeal to everyone, not just the religious. By doing so the reason for the holidays was buried beneath all the merchandise that is sold annually such as; colorful eggs, chocolate bunnies, candies, and baskets. These material things replaced Jesus, His symbolic cross and His resurrection. Most young kids who do not go to church would not recognize the significance of the Easter season. Even more atheists and non-believers are perfectly fine celebrating both Christmas and Easter because they feel they no longer have religious meanings, just borrowed pagan celebrations. During the Holidays employees are instructed not to say, *"Merry Christmas,"* or *"Happy Easter"* as not to offend anyone. These same businesses are more concerned with making a profit. They no longer sell merchandise with religious meaning. The closest thing to Jesus and God you might see will be angels and stars to decorate your light filled tree. There are no crosses, or pictures of Jesus to remind us of his birth. *"Happy Holidays"* became the only appropriate signs, and the only greeting heard at stores. Last year, 2009, a woman was fired from her retail job for refusing to remove her Keep Christ in Christmas pin. Employees are reluctantly forces to hold back their religious comments that were meant to inspire others during the holidays.

While writing this book a man was arrested and jailed for saying a prayer in school. As society continues to move in a direction away from Jesus, more and more of the meaning will diminish. Personally, I am afraid that in the future public confirmation of your belief will be criminal. Our nation will become *a "Don't Ask, Don't Tell"* society for fear of persecution. For two thousand years religions have struggled to be heard and to have free rights to practice. Now it seems we have reverted back to the dark time in history, where religious freedom will be replaced with religious persecution.

The History of the Trinity

The most commonly misunderstood Christian doctrine is the Holy Trinity, and the development thereof. Nowhere in the Holy Bible is the word trinity used to describe the three Gods as one. The concept of the trinity was not even made dogma until three hundred years after the death of Christ. It was never discussed amongst the disciples after His death. If they never regarded the three as one, then why do we? Where did the idea come from? And who believes it? The English word trinity is a derivative of the Latin word, *Trinitas,* meaning the number three, or triad. The noun form, *Trinus* means threefold or triple.

Ancient history reminds us that the trinity idea has been around for over two thousand years. The Father, the Son, and The Holy Spirit were not the first to be associated as one. It is believed that the origin of the trinity came from the Hindu belief which had the Brahmanical Triad. The triad consisted of Lord Brahma- Father God and Supreme Being creator of the universe, Vishnu- the preserver of the universe believed to have descended down to earth as a mortal to save mankind, and Shiva- the God of destruction. Together they represented the three powers of nature. Egyptian mythology had Osiris- an Egyptian God, Isis- his wife, and Horus-their son. Babylonian mythology had Nimrod, Semiramas, and Tammuz. In Israeli paganism it was Kether, Hokhamh, and Binah. The word trinity was not around to describe them, yet who they were and how they relate to each other is only similar, not exact to the Christian trinity.

Surely early church fathers and historians borrowed the concept and modified the understanding to help explain what they believed the scriptures were telling them. The first recorded account of the Father, the Son, and the Holy Spirit being referenced to as one person was by the Latin theologian, Tertullian, who wrote in the early third century. He writes;

> *"Thus the connection of the Father in the Son, and of the Son in the Paraclete, produces three coherent persons, who are yet distinct one from another. These Three are, one essence, not one person, as it is said, "I and my Father are One," in respect of unity of substance not singularity of number"* **210 A.D. (Against Praxeas, 25)**

I John 5:7, John 10:30
It was common for early Christian Leaders to quote Bible verses in defense of the trinity. Most notably is **John 10:30,**

"I and my father are One."

And the more debated **1 John 5:7,**

"For there are three that bear record in heaven, the Father, the Word, and the Holy Ghost: and these three are one."

1John 5:7 is shadowed in doubt about its Biblical authenticity. Generally it was believed to have been added somewhere in the middle ages. The mention verse is commonly referred to as, *"the comma"* and is contained in most translation of **1 John**. It was first published in the English Bible in 1522 A.D., owing its source to the third edition of the Textus Receptus (TR).

5:7 *"For there are three that bear record* **in heaven, the Father, the Word, and the Holy Ghost: and these three are one."* **5:8** *"And there*

are three that bear witness in earth, *the Spirit, and the water, and the* *blood: and these three agree in one.*"

The bold text is, "the comma," otherwise it is believed that the original Greek text reads as follows;

"For there are three that testify in heaven, the Spirit, and the water, and *the blood: and these three agree in one."*

Almost all of the ancient Greek manuscripts read the verse without the Comma, because of this, most modern Bibles such as the ESV, NIV, NRSV, and NASB omit the Comma altogether or have within their footnotes, *(not found in any Greek manuscripts before the sixteenth* *century.)*

There is plenty of historical evidence that shows our early church leaders reciting words that resemble the Comma more than one thousand years before it was believed to have been added. In 250 A.D., Cyprian of Carthage quotes John as saying,

> *"And again, of the Father, Son, and Holy Ghost it is* *written: "And the three are One."* **On the Lapsed, On** **the Novatians**

> *"The Lord says, "I and the Father are one,"* *and again it is* *written of the Father, and of the Son, and of the Holy Spirit,* *"and these three are one."* **On the Unity of the Church**

Cyprian had a habit of quoting scriptures and it is believed by some that the verse did appear in some even older ancient Greek manuscripts that were either lost or had been carelessly omitted by scribes. If one wants to doubt his quotes or the verses authenticity he would have to believe it was just a coincidence that he uses Father, Son and Holy Ghost more than thirteen hundred years before most believed it was added.

The very first known reference of **1 john 5:7** to appear in Epistle's text was in 380 A.D. in the Latin homily, *Liber Apologeticus.*

> *"As John says' and there are three which gives testimony on earth, the water, the flesh the blood, and these three are in one, and there are three which give testimony in heaven, the Father, the Word, and the Spirit, and these three are one in Christ Jesus."* **Liber Apologeticus.**

There is a trail of evidence that we find mentioning **1 John5:7** from about 200 A.D. through the 1500's. Here are just a few known references to the verse.

200 A.D.	Tertullian quotes the verse (Gill, *"An Exposition of The NT.)*
250 A.D.	Cyprian refers to the Comma (Vienna, vol.iii, p.215)
350 A.D.	Athanasius referred to the verse in *De Incarnatione.*
350 A.D.	Priscillian cites the verse (Vienna, vol. xviii, p.6)
450-530 A.D.	Three orthodox African writers quote the verse. Vigilius Tapensis, *"Three Witnesses in Heaven"* Victor Vitensis, *"Historia persecutionis"* Fulgentius, *"The three Heavenly Witnesses"*
500 A.D.	Cassiodorus cites the verse (MPL, vol. 70, col.1373)
550 A.D.	The "Speculum" contains the verse.
650 A.D.	Codex Pal Legionesis has the verse using instead *"in Jesus Christ."*
800 A.D.	Jerome's Vulgate has the verse.
1514 A.D.	Cardinal Ximenes' *Complutensian Polyglott* Greek edition contained the verse.

There are only eight known manuscripts of the Greek New Testaments out of thousands that contain the Comma. The oldest known Greek occurrence appears in a tenth century manuscript in the Bodleian Library. The Comma appears more in Latin manuscripts, even older sources such as the Codex Monacensis and the Speculum, both of the sixth-century.

John Gill commenting on **1 John 5:7,**

"As to the old Latin interpreter, it is certain it is to be seen in many Latin manuscripts of an early date, and stands in the Vulgate Latin edition of the London Polyglot Bible: and the Latin translation, which bears the name of Jerome, has it, and who, in an epistle of his to Eustochium, prefixed to his translation of these canonical epistles, complains of the omission of it by unfaithful interpreters."

"And as to its being wanting in some Greek manuscripts, as the Alexandrian, and others, it need only be said, that it is to be found in many others; it is in an old British copy, and in the Complutensian edition, the compilers of which made use of various copies; and OUT OF SIXTEEN ANCIENT COPIES OF ROBER STEPHEN'S, NINE OF THEM HAD IT." **Exposition of the Whole Bible (1746-1748)**

Matthew Henry on **1 John 5:7,**

"We are stopped in our course by the contest there is about the genuineness of v. 7. It is alleged that many old Greek manuscripts have it not. It should seem that the critics are not agreed what manuscripts have it and what not; nor do they sufficiently inform us of the integrity and value of the manuscripts they peruse...There are some rational surmises that seem to support the present text and reading."

"The seventh verse is very agreeable to the style and the theology of our apostle...Facundus acknowledges that Cyprian says that of his three it is written, Et hi tres unum sunt—and these three are one. NOW THESE ARE THE WORDS, NOT OF V. 8, BUT OF V. 7. They are not used concerning the three on earth, the Spirit, the water, and the blood; but the three in heaven, the Father, and the Word, and the Holy Ghost...If all the Greek manuscripts and ancient versions say concerning the Spirit, the water, and the blood, that in unum sunt—they agree in one, then it was not of them that Cyprian spoke, whatever variety there might be in the copies in his time, when he said it is written, unum sunt— they are one. And THEREFORE CYPRIAN'S WORDS SEEM STILL TO BE A FIRM TESTIMONY TO V. 7." **Matthew Henry's Complete Commentary**

John Calvin on **1 John5:7,**

"However, the passage flows better when this clause is added, and as I see that IT IS FOUND IN THE BEST AND MOST APPROVED COPIES, I am inclined to receive it as the true reading." **Commentary on the Catholic Epistles**

The historical evidence seems to suggest that it was the Latin speaking Churches and scribes that used the Comma. It eventually found its way into the Greek manuscripts and was then promptly removed as an attempt to preserve the integrity of the original ancient Greek text.

The New Testament is commonly referred to as the Greek New Testament because it was the ancient Greek text that was used as the foundation of the book. All the books were originally written in Koine Greek, although some claim that Matthew was written in either Hebrew or Aramaic. This is the reason there is debate over the integrity of **1 John**

5:7, because it does not appear in any of the original Greek manuscripts. History cannot ignore that the New Testament was translated in Latin, Syriac and Coptic. Rather **1 John 5:7** was an original lost from history or some scribes spin on translation, it does not change the others stance on the debate. It will not make someone lean one way or the other.

Some other scriptures to defend their idea regarding the trinity, which are vague and open for interpretation, are;

Luke 4:18, *"The spirit of the Lord is upon me."*

Matthew 28:19 *"Go ye therefore and teach all nations, baptizing them in the name of the father and of the son and of the Holy Ghost."*

2 Corinthians 13:14, *"The grace of the lord Jesus Christ and the love of God and the communion of the Holy Ghost be with you all. Amen."*

Here we have it from another point of view.

John 5:43, *"I am come in my father's name,"* (Jesus speaking)

John 14:26, *"But the comforter, which is the Holy Ghost, whom the father will send in my name."*

When read together the three separate verses give representation of a possible trinity while maintaining separate beings. There are an equal number of known verses that clearly declare God as only one person.

Zechariah 14:9, *"In this day shall there be one lord, and his name one."*

Luke 3:8, *"Thou shalt worship the Lord thy God, and him only shalt thou serve."*

Psalm 86:10, *"For thou art great, and doest wondrous things: thou art God alone."*

1 Corinthians 8:4, *"And that there is none other God but one."*

Mark 12:29, *"The Lord our God is one Lord."*

Isaiah 45:21, *"And there is no God else beside me; a just God and a savior; there is none besides me."*

Malachi 2:10, *"Have we not all one father? Hath not one God created us?"*

But how do the verses with only God and Jesus compare? Jesus, being God's only son would most definitely be in His likeness. But what is likeness? Likeness in the way He represents God and what God stands for as a divine spirit.

1 Corinthians 8:6, *"But to us there is but one God, the Father, of whom are all things, and we in him; and one Lord Jesus Christ, by whom are all things, and we by him."*

John 14:20, *"At that day ye shall know that I am in my father, and ye in me, and I in you."*

John 7:29, *"But I know him: for I am from him, and he hath sent me."*

John 8:29, *"And he that sent me is with me: the father hath not left me alone."*

John 14:11 *"Believe me that I am in the Father, and the Father in me."*

Just as a son will be in the likeness of his father both physically and spiritually, Jesus also talks about being the son of God in the same ways. The exact nature of Jesus to God will always be debated because of the vast number of scriptures that imply opposite meanings. There are scripture that show Jesus is separate from God and is acting on His own accord. **Matthew 27:43,** *"I am the son of God."*

John 5:37, *"And the Father himself, which hath sent me."*

1 Timothy 2:5, *"For there is one God, and one mediator between God and man, and the man is Christ Jesus."*

John 16:10, *"Because I go to my Father."*

John 20:17, *"Touch me not: for I am not yet ascended to my Father."*

Luke 23:46, *"Father, into thy hands I commend my spirit."*

Holy Spirit, Holy Ghost

How does the Holy Spirit fit in with God and Jesus? The Spirit appears in more verses with God than Jesus, that is the Holy Spirit is in God Alone. **Isaiah 48:16,** *"There am I and now the Lord God, and his spirit, has sent me."*

John 4:24, *"God is a spirit: and they that worship him must worship him in spirit and in truth."*

Matthew 3:16, *"And Jesus, when he was baptized, went up straightway out, of the water: and, lo, the Heavens were open unto him, and he saw the spirit of God descend like a dove and lighting upon him."*

If the Holy Spirit is in God alone, why does he have it? He most likely uses the Holy Spirit as a way to make himself visible to people because He has no form and cannot be seen.

John 1:18, *"No man hath seen God at any time."*

John 5:37, *"Ye have neither heard his voice at any time, nor seen his shape."*

1 Timothy 1:17, *"Now unto the King eternal, immortal, invisible, the only wise God."*

Why do we see scriptures with the Holy Ghost? Just as every mortal has a spirit, Jesus too had a spirit. The accepted definition of a ghost not relating to the Bible is the soul of a man after he dies or the spirit of a man that left the body. When the body dies the spirit or ghost is released. His spirit was given to Him from God, but was it of God and called the Holy Ghost? His disciples refer to the teachings of the Holy Ghost after He dies. The term Holy Ghost can only be found in the New Testament and it is used ninety times. The Holy Ghost is introduced to Jesus in **Matthew 1:20,** *"Joseph, thou son of David fear not to take unto thee Mary thy wife: for that which is conceived in her is of the Holy Ghost."*

Other related verses regarding the Holy Ghost are;

Matthew 12:31, *"But the blasphemy against the Holy Ghost shall not be forgiven unto men."*

Luke 3:22, *"And the Holy Ghost descended in a bodily shape like a dove upon him, and a voice came from heaven, which said, Thou art my beloved son."*

Acts 1:8, *"But ye shall receive power, after that the Holy Ghost is come upon you."*

1 Corinthians 2:13, *"Which things also we speak, not in the words which man's wisdom teacheth, but which the Holy Ghost teacheth."*

I believe that the Holy Spirit and the Holy Ghost are separate, each being divine with either Jesus or God. Jesus is equal to the Holy Ghost as God is equal to the Holy Spirit. The translators intentionally used Ghost and Spirit separately as a way to distinguish Jesus' divinity from God's divinity. If the Ghost and Spirit are one in the same there should be consistent usage of either Ghost or Spirit in the KJV Bible, not both.

To further explore the reason for the specific word usage we need to understand the words that were first translated. The Greek word πνεῦμα translated as *pneuma* (pnyoo'-mah) means wind, spirit and ghost. It is derived from the original Greek root word *pneo* having various word meanings such as; breath, breeze, spirit and soul. In the New Testament you see a consistent usage of the word *pneuma* for both ghost and spirit.

Luke 4:1, *"And Jesus being full of the Holy Ghost (pneuma) returned from Jordan, and was led by the Spirit (pneuma) into the wilderness."*

In Hebrew there are two separate words for spirit and ghost. Some theologians believe that the Hebrew word עַוֹגַ, gava pronounced (gaw-vah') means both spirit and ghost. In fact it only means to expire, perish and die. Gava was used in translation because it was used in reference to when someone is dying. The Hebrew word for spirit is *ruach*, pronounced (roo'akh). Its original meaning varies as; air, breath, wind and spirit. The correct word usage depended on how it was used in relation to a person, an event or the act of.

In modern Bibles such as the New King James Version (NKJV), New International Version (NIV), New American Standard Bible (NASB), New Living Translation (NLT) and several others they revised the scriptures by changing ghost to spirit. Probably as a way to better defend the trinity belief.

Matthew 3:11 KJV, *"I indeed baptize you with water unto repentance: but He that cometh after me is mightier than I, whose shoes I am not worthy to bear: He shall baptize you with the Holy Ghost, and with fire."* NKJV, *"I indeed baptize you with water unto repentance, but He who is coming after me is mightier that I, whose sandals I am not worthy to carry, He will baptize you with the Holy Spirit and fire."*

Acts 1:2 KJV, *"Until the day in which he was taken up, after that he through the Holy Ghost had given commandments unto the apostles whom* *he had chosen.*"NIV, *"Until the day he was taken up to heaven, after giving instructions through the Holy Spirit to the apostles he had chosen."*

Luke 3:22 KJV, *"And the Holy Ghost descended in a bodily shape like a dove upon Him, and a voice came from Heaven, which said, Thou art my beloved; in the I am well pleased."* NASB, *"And the Holy Spirit descended upon Him in a bodily form like a Son; in thee I am well pleased."* dove, and a voice came out of Heaven. You are my beloved Son, in you I am well-pleased."*

John 7:39 KJV, *"For the Holy Ghost was not yet given; because that Jesus was not yet glorified."* NLT, *"But the Holy Spirit had not yet been given, because Jesus had not yet entered into his glory."*

In verses that use the phrase, *"giving up the ghost"* which simply means to pass away, they intentionally removed the term replacing it with either *"death"* or *"passed away."* In other verses they replaced ghost with spirit, doing the opposite injustice to scriptures. An example of that can be found in **Matthew 27:50** KJV,

"Jesus, when he had cried again with a loud voice, yielded up the ghost." NLT, *"But the spirit had not yet been given because Jesus had not yet entered into His glory."*

These examples further defend the notion that the Bible is the word of man, inspired by God, and represents how man intentionally changed the words in scriptures to accommodate changes in culture and belief.

Church Councils defend the Trinity
In 325 A.D., during the Council of Nicaea, Constantine with the help of bishops established the doctrine of the trinity as orthodox and adapted the Nicene Creed to describe them using, *"being of one substance."* These

words solidified the understanding of the Father, the Son and the Holy Spirit as the trinity. In February 380 A.D., Emperor Theodosius decrees Christianity as the state religion of the Empire and the church must adhere to Trinitarianism. 415 A.D., The Council of Carthage refers to **1 John 5:7** as a basic text proving the doctrine while contending with the Arians anti–trinity belief. To further clarify the doctrine on the trinity there was another church council called in 451 A.D. The Council of Chalcedon convened to define the two natures of Jesus as both divine and human. The controversy arose from the false teaching that Jesus had only one nature called, Monophysitism. It was taught by the Abbot Eutyches, who was later excommunicated from the church.

For centuries the formation and development of the faith was in the churches hand. Every dogma and Christian belief was developed from hundreds of years of debates and church councils. To this day there are debates over the trinity and other beliefs. Until God comes down to explain it we will be left with our own theories to explain what we cannot understand.

Trinitarianism is the belief in the trinity, which God exists in three persons being as one substance; The Father, the Son, and The Holy Ghost. You would think that a Christian doctrine developed to express an understanding would be practiced by all divisions of Christianity. The problem is that when the concept was developed there was only one church, (the Catholic Church) that agreed upon and accepted the dogma. Two thousand years later as divisions occurred and beliefs were reevaluated, changed, and rejected to fit newly formed Christian faiths, the dogma was challenged. By doing so the creditability of new churches and divisions were also challenged. What was considered orthodox changed to unorthodox while still maintaining Christian status. Some Christian churches are often viewed as heretics for not following the trinity dogma as established by the Catholic Church. The divisions of Christianity that continue to practice the dogma of the trinity are the Eastern Orthodox, Roman Catholicism, and some groups emerging from the Protestant Reformation, such as Anglican, Methodist, Lutheran, and Presbyterian.

The contradictions of Trinitarianism are both Binitarianism and Unitarianism. Binitarianism is the belief of one deity in two persons and Unitarianism is simply the belief in one person. Similar to Unitarianism is Modalism also called, Sabellianism.

Modalism is the complete denial of the trinity. The two noted leaders in the Modalism movement were Praxeas and a Libyan priest named Sabellius, who came to Rome toward the end of Zephyrinus's reign (198-217 A.D.). Sabellius was later condemned as a heretic in 220 A.D. by the Roman bishop Callistus. Those who practice it believe God existed as three manifested modes at different times. This belief was condemned as heresy by both Tertullian and Dionysis, bishop of Rome in 262 A.D. Dionysius writes in his Against the Sabellians paragraph 3,

> *"That admirable and divine unity, therefore, must neither be separated into three divinities, nor must the dignity and eminent greatness of the Lord be diminished by having applied to it the name of creation, but we must believe on God the Father Omnipotent, and on Christ Jesus His Son, and on the Holy Spirit. Moreover, that the Word is united to the God of all, because He says, "I and the Father are one;" and, "I am in the Father, and the Father is in Me." Thus doubtless will be maintained in its integrity the doctrine of the divine Trinity, and the sacred announcement of the monarchy."*

Hippolytus writes in 205 A.D.

> *"If, again, Noetus alleges Christ's own words when he said, "I and the Father are one," let him attend to the fact and understand that He did not say, "I and the Father am one, but are one." For the word "are" is not said of one person. Rather, it refers to two persons, but one power. Christ has Himself made this clear, when He spoke to His Father*

concerning the disciples: "The glory which you gave me I have given them that they may be one." **Ibid., vol. 5.226; cf. Hippolytus,** Against Noetus

Defending the Trinity, **Gregory Thaumaturgus** (the Wonderworker; 260 A.D.) speaks of Sabellius in.

"But some treat the Holy Trinity in an awful manner, when they confidently assert that there are not three persons, and introduce (the idea of) a person devoid of subsistence. Wherefore we clear ourselves of Sabellius, who says that the Father and the Son are the same [Person] . . ."We forswear this, because we believe that three persons-namely, Father, Son, and Holy Spirit-are declared to possess the one Godhead: for the one divinity showing itself forth according to nature in the Trinity establishes the oneness of the nature." **Gregory Thaumaturgus A Sectional Confession of Faith 7, in ANF, vol. 6.**

Cyril of Jerusalem writes in 348 A.D., in his *Catechetical Lectures* also defending the trinity.

"For the Only-begotten Son of God said plainly to the Apostles, Go ye, and make disciples of all the nations, baptizing them into the name of the Father, and of the Son, and of the Holy Ghost. Our hope is in Father, and Son, and Holy Ghost. We preach not three Gods; let the Marcionites be silenced; but with the Holy Ghost through One Son, we preach One God. . . . We neither separate the Holy Trinity, like some; nor do we as Sabellius work confusion." **Cyril of Jerusalem** Catechetical Lectures **16.4, in** NPNF; **vol. 7, 2nd series.**

Ignatius of Antioch in 107 A.D. speaks out in defense of the trinity he writes,

> *"Jesus Christ, who was with the Father before the beginning of time, and in the end was revealed. . . . He, being begotten by the Father before the beginning of time, was God the Word, the only-begotten Son, and remains the same forever"*
> **Ignatius Letter to the Magnesians 6, in ANF, vol.1**

The singular belief, the view that they are three separate beings who are only one in function, not one in divinity, is believed by some Pentecostal groups, and the Church of Jesus Christ of Latter-day Saints. Some Christian groups are stuck in the middle, believing in all three but only two are connected in spirit, either Jesus and Spirit, or Holy Ghost or God and Spirit.

Whether you accept the trinity or not is a decision you will have to make. No matter which way you go the decision would not do an unjust to God.

Trust in the word of God not man

As Christians we were always taught that the Bible is the word of God and therefore must be trusted. We should always trust God first, because His words were first before man intervened.

Psalm 56:11, *"In God have I put my trust: I will not be afraid what man can do unto me."*

Psalm 118:8, *"It is better to trust the Lord than to put confidence in man."*

Proverbs 3:5 *"Trust in the Lord with all thine heart."*

Proverbs 30:5, *"Every word of God is pure: he is a shield unto them that put their trust in him."*

1 Corinthians 2:5, *"That your faith should not stand in the wisdom of men, but in the power of God."*

Why did the development of Christianity move into the hands of man instead of us following the scriptures? For one, man is the reason that we have scriptures to follow. With Jesus and His disciples gone, man was forced to carry the torch and guide Christians toward God, yet somewhere along the way the meaning was lost in the dark. What we came to believe was made by man and not by God. Even though the trinity is a church made concept; it was done so with the best interest in mind. No matter what anyone will tell you about the trinity in the Bible, remember Jesus never taught about the three godheads. He also never said that He, God and the Holy Spirit are one in the same. The trinity is by far the hardest of all Biblical canons to understand. References in the Bible to a trinity of divine beings are vague, at best. Whichever way you feel I urge you to read and study the Bible and decide for yourself where your beliefs fit in.

Chapter 6:
Living the Christian Life

"And the burden of the Lord shall ye mention no more: for every man's word shall be his burden; for ye have perverted the words of the living God."
Jeremiah 23:26

One Sunday while at Church, my pastor delivered a great sermon. She preached, *"The Greatest Commandment."* As I sat listening and absorbing her words, she opened my mind about my faith. I was always wondering, what it would take for Christianity as a whole to unite once again. Every division of Christianity will preach to you what it means to live a Christian life. Belief and practices vary greatly, you can easily get lost within the vast degrees of morality that each represent. This would be a better world and religion if everyone agreed on a few simple points. Love one another, love the Lord our God, and live your life like you are in *"The Kingdom of Heaven."* Everything within the Bible can be summed up with these three points which cover the basics of living the Christian life.

Love one another. It is easier said than done. One of the key points to being a good Christian is not to look upon others with bias and judgment.

Matthew 7:1-2, *"Judge not, that ye be not judged. For with what judgment ye judge, ye shall be judged."*

It doesn't matter, what color, sex, race, age or religion. We are all equal in God's eye; therefore we must live as though God's eyes are on us at all times.

Mark 12:30-31, *"And thou shalt love the Lord thy God with all thy heart, and with all thy soul, and with all thy mind, and with all thy strength; this is the first commandments, and the second is like namely this, Thou shalt love thy neighbor as thyself. There is none other commandments greater than these."*

Loving thy neighbor as thyself is such an important commandment that it is mentioned in numerous verses in both the Old Testament and New Testament.

Leviticus 19:18, *"Thou shalt not avenge, nor bear any grudge against the children of thy people, but thou shalt love thy neighbor as thyself: I am the Lord."*

Matthew 19:19, *"Thy shalt love thy neighbor as thyself."*

But does it mean neighbor literally? Neighbor would be the obvious including your fellow man and even your enemies.

Matthew 5:44, *"But I say unto you, Love your enemies, bless them that curse you."*

If we are to represent Jesus we need to follow His example. Jesus loved everyone, even those that did not believe and those who persecuted Him.

Mark 3:35, *"For whosoever shall do the will of God, the same is my brother, and my sister, and mother."*

Clearly to be in Jesus' family we must live *God like* in our thought and actions. I believe the goal of living a Christian life is to immolate Jesus. He maintains His moral stance in the face of opposition and despair. This standard of morality is almost impossible for mortals to immolate today.

What type of life did Jesus live? If you sit back and read and analyze every aspect of the life of Jesus you will make up your own mind on what He stood for. Jesus as a mortal owned nothing of monetary value with the exception of the clothes on His back. He traveled and witnessed to all people of the land. He did not go door to door and ask people to join; instead He welcomed those that came to follow Him. When word got around that a man of God could perform miracles people flocked toward him out of curiosity. What did He represent? How can we follow? Jesus said in **Matthew 4:19,**

"Follow me and I will make you fishers of men."

John 8:12, *"I am the light of the world: he that followeth me shall not walk in darkness, but shall have the light of life."*

Mark 8:34, *"Whosoever will come after me, let him deny himself, and take up his cross, and follow me."*

Jesus knew that to follow Him meant they will be persecuted, denied and hated.

Luke 21:16-17, *"And ye shall be betrayed both by parents, and brethren, and kinsfolks, and friends: and some of you shall they cause to be put to death. And ye shall be hated of all men for my name's sake."*

Jesus as the son of God was one with God. God created man in his image; therefore we are the image of God, and Jesus. In Genesis when Adam and Eve ate from the tree of knowledge of good and evil human kind became gods.

Genesis 3:5, *"For God doth know that in the day ye eat thereof, then your eyes shall be opened, and ye shall be as gods, knowing good and evil."*

Genesis 3:22, *"And the Lord God said, behold the man is become as one of us."*

John 10:34, *"Ye are Gods."*

1 Peter 1:15-16, *"But as he which hath called you is holy, so be holy in all manner of conversation; because it is written, be ye holy: for I am holy."*

Leviticus 19:2, *"Speak unto all the congregation of the children of Israel, and say unto them, ye shall be holy: for I the Lord your God am holy."*

To be Holy as Jesus is being held at a higher standard of morality, and consciousness. Everyone was born, to have within them, the ability to live great lives of morality, and spiritual discipline. Exercising such rites is very difficult, and to achieve such results requires one to be at their very best at all times.

The Kingdom of Heaven

Jesus completely destroyed the stereotypical idea of a kingdom that most people had at that time. Part of the reason He was killed was because of that idea. If He was from the blood line of King David and The King of the Jews, surely He would have fit the image of a king they have been building up for so long. A king is powerful, wears a white robe, adorned in gold and jewels, protected by an army, has a great temple and is loved by his followers. Jesus only had followers, there were rumors of His powers and He did not fit the image. Jesus, over time, proved that He was a king and the son of God. His actions were king like, it that He loved everyone and took care of those in need; never turning His back on anyone. Jesus tells His disciples and others about the Kingdom of Heaven throughout the four gospels. It was prophesized that a king would come from the blood line of King David and save the chosen people.

Jeremiah 23: 5, *"Behold, the days come, saith the Lord, that I will raise unto David a righteous Branch, and a King shall reign and prosper, and shall execute judgment and justice in the earth."*

The Kingdom of God was at hand the moment Jesus was born.

Luke 1:32-33, *"He shall be great, and shall be called the Son of the Highest: and the Lord shall give unto him the throne of His father David: And He shall reign over the house of Jacob for ever; and of His kingdom there shall be no end."*

The Kingdom of God is believed to be a place where we go when we die. It is our final resting place for being a good Christian on earth. But if Jesus was a king and alive here on Earth, would it not make sense for it to be His kingdom at that time. Jesus refers to the Kingdom of God as currently at hand while He was living. A kingdom is nothing without a king and therefore could not exist.

Mark 1:15, *"The time is fulfilled, and the Kingdom of God is at hand: repent ye, and believe the gospel."*

And in **Matthew 10:7,** *"And as ye go preach, saying, The Kingdom of Heaven is at hand."*

Maybe Jesus was preaching The Kingdom of God as a way for us to live each day. Surely living an ethical and moral life following Jesus would guarantee us our place in the Kingdom of Heaven. Some believe it is just that simple. You cannot get to heaven on deeds alone. Without accepting Jesus as your Savior and having complete faith in Him we cannot go anywhere. We should be living this life as a way to prepare for the next life. Jesus undoubtedly knew the troubles facing men and mans inability to grasp bigger things. He spent His last years teaching His disciples, preparing them to go out and spread God's words. Later in His life Jesus came to understand how man's troubles were great and their lack of trust combined with the unwillingness to follow will lead men to suffer.

John 18:36, *"My kingdom is not of this world: if my kingdom were of this world, then would my servants fight, that I should not be delivered to the Jews: but now is my kingdom not from hence."*

Jesus further warns man of their behavior and how it will prevent them from eternal life. Paul writes in **1 Corinthians 6:10,**

"For thieves, nor covetous, nor drunkards, nor revilers, nor extortioners, shall inherit the Kingdom of God."

Obviously someone who lives a life of sin would not enter the Kingdom of God, nor are they living like they are in the Kingdom of Heaven. The Kingdom of God can be interpreted different ways. Is it literally a place or a metaphor, or is it something else? Could the Kingdom of God be just a state of mind as opposed to a physical place?

Mark 10:15, *"Verily I say unto you, whosoever shall not received the Kingdom of God as a little child, he shall not enter therein."*

How one does received the Kingdom of God as a little child?

Baptized into the Kingdom of God

> **Galatians 3:27,** *"For as many of you as have been Baptized into Christ have put on Christ."*

Living in the Kingdom of God could simply mean the act of baptism. When you are baptized you are cleansed of sin, you accept Jesus Christ as your savior and follow Him.

John 3:3-5, *"Jesus answered and said unto him, Verily, verily, I say unto thee, Except a man be born again, he cannot see the kingdom of God. Nicodemus saith unto him, how can a man be born when he is old? Can he enter the second time into his mother's womb, and be born? Jesus answered, Verily, verily, I say unto thee, except a man be born of water and of the Holy Spirit, he cannot enter into the Kingdom of God."*

John clearly states that one must be *"born of water and of the Holy Spirit,* "(baptism) to receive the Kingdom of God. The first time we are born we are born physically in water. The symbolic meaning of baptism is to prepare us for a second life in the Kingdom of God. Jesus commands all believers to do the same act. Therefore Jesus becomes our king and we become the citizens of His kingdom. What exactly does a baptism entail? Baptize is a translation of the Greek word *batizw.* Its root word is *baptw* a term used in the early first century expressing the act of both cleansing and changing the color of cloth. Both cleansing and changing symbolized the effect baptism has on ones soul. Baptism is an outward sign of an inward cleansing.

1 Peter 3:21, *"The like figure whereunto even baptism doth also now save us (not the putting away of the filth of the flesh, but the answer of a good conscience toward God,) by the resurrection of Jesus Christ."*

The origin of our baptism tradition can be found in the New Testament. In Hebrew baptism is referred to as a *doctrine* indicating its importance's to the early church.

Hebrews 6:2, *"Of the doctrine of baptisms, and of laying hands."*

We know that as early as 64 A.D. the practice has been well established by Christians as a way of accepting Jesus. To be baptized one has to be immersed in water by another Christian. This act was made famous by John the Baptist, who was Jesus' older cousin and the one who baptized Him.

Matthew 3:13-15, *"Then cometh Jesus from Galilee to Jordan unto John, to be baptized of him. But John forbad him, saying, I have need to be baptized of thee, and comest thou to me? And Jesus answering said unto him, suffer it to be so now: for thus it becometh us to fulfill all righteousness."*

As tradition goes you are immediately baptized when you have accepted Jesus for salvation. These acts are generally tied together.

Acts 8:12, *"But when they believed, they were baptized, both men and women."*

Acts 2:41, *"Then they that gladly received his word were baptized: and the same day there were added unto them about three thousand souls."*

Acts 9:18, *"And immediately there fell from his eyes as it had been scales: and he received sight forthwith, and arose, and was baptized."*

Acts 16:30-33, *"And brought them out, and said, Sirs, what must I do to be saved? And they said, Believed on the Lord Jesus Christ, and thou shalt be saved, and thy house. And they spake unto him the word of the Lord, and to all that were in his house. And he took them the same hour of the night, and washed their stripes; and was baptized, he and all his straightway."*

Clearly the Bible promotes baptism as an outward sign of accepting Jesus. This public act of cleansing is also a public confession that enables us to start a new life as Christians who have accepted Jesus as our Savior.

Many of our greatest church fathers of the early third and fourth centuries were not baptized until they were adults, even though being born into a Christian family. Of them is St. Basil the Great, St. Augustine and St. Jerome. Some later in life like St. Augustine became advocates for baptizing infants convince of the original sin doctrine that was develop by the church. Of them are St. John Chrysostom, St. Ambrose, and St. Cyril of Alexandria.

But what if someone dies as an adult and was never baptized does he go to heaven? According to the teaching of Jesus the answer is yes. Remember the story of the two thieves crucified with Jesus. One had accepted Him, because he believed and had faith in Jesus. They did not stop the crucifixion so he could be baptized and yet Jesus promised him paradise in His kingdom. It is more than baptism that saves, it is having faith in Jesus that gives you salvation.

If the purpose of baptism is for the remission (washing away) of sins

Acts 2:38, *"Then Peter said unto them, Repent, and be baptized every one of you in the name of Jesus Christ for the remission of sins, and ye shall receive the gift of the Holy Ghost."*

Acts 22:16, *"Arise, and be baptized, and wash away thy sins, calling on the name of the Lord,"*

Why was Jesus baptized if He was free of sin? When Jesus met John at the river Jordan there was a multitude of people who wanted to be baptized to show they were sorry for their sins and to reconnect with God. Jesus showed His will to be part of the community of Jews who wanted nothing more than to renew their relationship with God. As a practicing Jew it was important for Jesus to uphold Jewish tradition. Traditions such as observing the Passover, upholding Jewish law and the act of cleansing were practiced by those Jews who were committed to God. The baptism of Jesus symbolized the start of His three year mission to spread the word of God and it further established the traditional act required of cleansing yourself of sins, to be saved to enter the Kingdom of God.

Baptizing Infants (The Doctrine of Original Sin)

To make the decision to accept Jesus and follow Him you will have to have a clear understanding of right, (good) and wrong, (evil). You will have to be at an age in which you commit to a decision and mature enough to deal with the consequences of your actions. Where did the idea of *"original sin"* or *"ancestral sin"* come from? It started in the second century with Bishop of Lyon Irenaeus. He was struggling with the Gnostics teachings and their ideas of Jesus. He believed that every man is born into a fallen world due to the fall of Adam in the Garden of Eden. Later in the early 400 A.D. Augustine of Hippo from North Africa, (354-430A.D.) developed the doctrine of original sin from Irenaeus' belief. His doctrine would define the belief as held by the Orthodox Church. He most likely used Paul's epistle to the Romans as a foundation of his theology.

Romans 5:12-14, *"Wherefore, as by one man sin entered into the world, and death by sin; and so death passed upon all men, for that all have sinned: For until the law sin was in the world: but sin is not imputed when there is no law."*

In his letter to the Corinthians Paul writes that because of Adam all men are dead, (spiritually) because of sin.

1 Corinthian 15:22, *"For as in Adam all die."*

Augustine's theology is that we inherited our sins from the very origin of all sins. At birth we are born with sin committed by Adam and therefore we are separate from God. Since sin is rooted in all human existence we must be cleansed of sin to accept Jesus. With the doctrine established within the Roman Catholic Church, who views original sin as a condition in which humans are born, parents began to be concerned with the fate of their children. He preached that all unbaptized infants, if they die, will go to hell. They had to be baptized for the *"remission of sin."* Wanting to be right with God, parents wanted their infants baptized to save them. The decision was then made to sprinkle water on their forehead to avoid the risk of immersing them.

St. Fulgentius of Ruspe, (462 or 467-January 1, 533 A.D.) was a devote follower of St. Augustine's ideals, and a bishop of the city of Ruspe, Africa. He wrote,

> *"Hold most firmly and by no means doubt that little children, whether they die before or after birth, pass, without the holy sacrament of baptism, from this world, to be punished with the everlasting punishment of eternal fire."* **Paganism and Christianity, J.A. Farrer p. 48-49**

By no means do their views represent the ideals of baptism as held by the whole of Christianity.

There are no verses in the Bible were infants are baptized. Are young children then doomed to hell for sins they never committed? The answer is no. Infants and young children are not held responsible for the sins of their parents. This idea is clearly preached in the Bible.

Ezekiel 18:19-20, *"Yet say ye, why? Doth not the son bear the iniquity of the father? When the son hath done that which is lawful and right, and hath done them, he shall surely live. The soul that sinneth, it shall die. The son shall not bear the iniquity of the father."*

Luke 18:16, *"Suffer little children to come unto me, and forbid them not, for of such is the kingdom of God."*

Deuteronomy 24:16, *"The father shall not be put to death for the children, neither shall the children be put to death for the fathers: every man shall be put to death for his own sin."*

In the Old Testament book of Isaiah, he writes that children will sin without knowing better, until they reach the age of understanding and learn God.

Isaiah 29:23-24, *"But when he seeth his children, the work of mine hands, in the midst of him, they shall sanctify my name, and sanctify the Holy One of Jacob, and shall fear the God of Israel. They also that erred in spirit shall come to understanding, and they that murmured shall learn doctrine."*

In Genesis God acknowledges that children, from their youth are capable of evil, not from when they were born or infants.

Genesis 8:21, *"Imagination of man's heart is evil from his youth."*

Children are innocent until they understand right from wrong. Neither God nor Jesus will hold children accountable for what they cannot understand.

The second Council of Orange in 529 A.D. convened to defend Augustine's doctrine of original sin. The main purpose was to deal with the ongoing debates between the teaching of Augustine and Pelagius, a British monk who lived from 354-420/440 A.D. Pelagius challenged traditional church view and the doctrine of original sin as presented by Augustine. Pelagius held that humans were born innocent without any sin. Since we were made in the image of God we were made with no sin. God gave us free will and with that we decided to sin or live a moral life. The council agreed with Augustine's view of total depravity, original sin. They declared his views as orthodox and established church canons to firmly uphold the church's position

> **CANON2.** *"If anyone asserts that Adam's sin affected him alone and not his descendents also, or at least if he declares that it is only the death of the body which is the punishment for sin, and not also that sin, which is the death of the soul,*

passed through one man to the whole human race, he does injustice to God and contradicts the Apostle, who says, "Therefore as sin came into the world through one man and death through sin, and so death spread to all men because all men sinned" **(Roman 5:12)**

And from the book, **Catechism of the Catholic Church**, **416-418** we read.

"By his sin, Adam, as the first man, lost the original holiness and justice he had received from God, not only for himself but for all humans. Adam and Eve transmitted to their descendants human nature wounded by their own first sin and hence deprived of original holiness and justice; this deprivation is called "original sin". As a result of original sin, human nature is weakened in its powers, subject to ignorance, suffering and the domination of death, and inclined to sin (this inclination is called "concupiscence")

Followers of the doctrine include Protestant reformers such as Martin Luther, John Calvin and some churches from within Roman Catholicism. They believed that all humans inherited their sinful nature from the fall of Adam and therefore are alienated from God until they are baptized. Most churches such as Churches of Christ, Christian Churches, the Disciples of Christ and Church of Jesus Christ of Latter-day Saints, known as Mormons, reject the doctrine of original sin. They believe infants and little children are not held accountable for their parent's sins and are not capable of sinning until they reach the age of accountability.

Trouble Teachings

Matthew 15:7-9, *"Ye hypocrites, well did Esaias prophesy of you, saying. This people draweth nigh unto me with their mouth, and honouerth me with their lips; but their heart is far from me."*

Mark 7:7-8, *"Howbeit in vain do they worship me, teaching for doctrines the commandments of men. For laying aside the commandment of God, ye hold the tradition of men, as the washing of pots and cups: and many other such like things ye do."*

There are some Christian teachings that have been heavily considered as false. False teachings are hard to imagine from people claiming to be followers of Christ, yet some feel compelled to create false beliefs knowing that it is not God's will. If Jesus Christ did not teach them what gives us the right to decide what to follow? The first, up for debate, is *once saved always saved,* a popular teaching by some Southern Baptists churches. The theory they developed is that, once you are saved you stay saved. To first understand the teaching you have to know what being saved really means to some. Are they reciting words thinking it's that easy to go to heaven? Or are they really saved from at deeply personal level having established a close relationship with God that will never end. If the second one is true, then yes that person is saved. Again, a belief that has come from Bible scriptures used to establish faith.

Acts 2:21, *"Whosoever shall call on the name of the Lord shall be saved."*

The idea of this being a false teaching depends upon your understanding and what you perceive as truth.

The followers of this false teaching (if they believe the first) strongly believe and will argue to defend it. They are convinced they are forever saved and no matter what they do they are guaranteed a spot in the Kingdom of Heaven. Another church that takes this idea to the extreme is *Growing in Grace International Ministries, Inc* located in Doral, Florida. Their leader Jose Luis De Jesus Miranda preaches his motto, *"salvo siempre salvo"* or *"once saved always saved."* He teaches his congregation that both sin and the devil were destroyed when Jesus died on the cross. He continues with, *"once you are saved you can no longer do evil in the eyes of God, you are forever his children."*

His followers are so convinced in his words that some get *"SSS"* tattooed on the necks, arms or legs, as a sign of dedication to their leader. This is a troubled practice for it takes away the meaning of living the Christian life. The idea is absurd and the majority of Christians view it as unorthodox.

Just say a Prayer

Some pastors from evangelical churches preach about the power of prayer. They believe that what you pray for you will get. This is a very dangerous proposition to instill on desperate Christians seeking help from God. The idea was taken as literal from the verses of;

Matthew 7:7-8, *"Ask, and it shall be given you seek, and ye shall find; knock, and it shall be opened unto you; For every one that asketh receiveth; and he that seeketh findeth; and to him that knocketh, it shall be opened."*

Matthew 21:22, *"And all things, whatsoever ye shall ask in prayer, believing, ye shall received."*

Mark 11:24, *"Therefore I say unto you, what things so ever ye desire, when ye pray, believed that ye received them, and ye shall have them."*

What if someone had prayed for God to heal a loved one from cancer? They pray every day with hope in sincere faith that their prayer would be answered. Their loved one still dies from the disease. Whose fault is it? Evangelist would say it was the fault of the person praying for their prayers were not sincere, or they did not pray hard enough. That would be more guilt than most people could bear, that is if they believe this teaching. The actual story behind the verses is that Jesus would take care of His children. Just like a father looking out for and providing for his children so does Jesus.

In the past I had people approach me and asked for me to pray their special needs. Whether it was a sick family member, marital problems or financial problems that has burden them, prayer is their last resort. It seems some Christians get a cozy comfortable feeling knowing that someone is praying for their needs, and because of that prayer everything will be fine. Those that have approached me call themselves Christians, but I know from their lifestyle and how they act that they do not hold true to their Christian faith. Calling yourself a Christian is to easy of a title to claim, and maybe to some it sold be earned. The idea that God will answer my prayer or for some reason favor me because of my devote faith, or because I am a deacon, appears good enough a reason to have me pray for them and give them a sense of false hope. I tell them all the same, *"what have you done to better yourself, God will not help those who do not help themselves."* Consider these two stories regarding the power of prayer.

There was a Christian man who was heavily burdened with financial hardship. He prayed to God to win the lottery. Every week he prayed and prayed, he got more and more desperate with each prayer to the point of begging to be the winner. One night while in deep prayer begging for God to solve all of his own troubles he heard a voice say, "Give me a break, buy a ticket."

There was a Christian man who set forth to go fishing early one morning. As the day went the weather turned, it became cloudy with rough waters. Suddenly and without warning a rogue wave hit his boat capsizing him into the water. The event happened suddenly, he was unable to prepare and was without communication and life preserver. He struggled to flit back his boat, but was unable to do so since he went alone that day. For hours he treaded water trying to stay afloat. Hours more went by without prevail, no boats in sight to help. Feeling exhausted and to his end he thought of his wife and kids at home, who had no idea of his perilous situation. Not knowing if he will live he made a desperate prayer. "God I am sorry for my life and lack of faith. I am sorry for not being the best Christian I can, and not thinking of others. Please if you can find it in you give me one last chance, I promise I will change." Another hour went buy when suddenly he noticed off in the distant a boat. He tried as hard as he could to make enough noise as to be heard by this other fishing vessel. Finally he saw the boat turn and slowly head his way, he got the attention of the owner. The Good Samaritan threw him a life vest and rescued the poor man after what seemed like an eternity in the water. While being lifted into the boat he caught a glimpse at the boat's name, Last Chance.

Easy Believism

Easy believism or *non-Lord salvation* is a popular view that one has to only believe to be saved and there is no need for discipleship. *Carnal Christians* is a common term used to describe someone who made the decision to accept Jesus but does not practice the faith. This free-grace is viewed as an easy out for Christians who only want to accept Jesus with no commitment to His message. This idea of living as a carnal Christian has conjured up many debates and only a small portion of Christians follow.

> *"Today, in the ranks of our Independent Baptist churches, we are overcome by the super salesmen 'soulwinners' who pull professions out of lost souls with a promise that they will go to heaven on the basis of a little prayer and a profession of faith in Jesus. They follow the Hyles, Hutson, Gray, Vineyard, statement of faith and never know the reality of passing from death to life. The followers of these preachers of corruption are promising lost soul's liberty where there is not liberty. . . . One "Easy-Believism" preacher, Jack*

Hyles of the large First Baptist Church of Hammond, Indiana, says that 'sin does not have to be repented of, only forgotten.'... I am afraid these preachers want to hide their sins instead of forget them." **Gaylon Wilson**

"Easy believism' is mosty propagated by the Charismatic movement and the 'Christian' Rock movement. 'Easy believism' makes everyone a Christian that both speaks in tongues or simply shows up to some kind of a religious meeting and waves their hands around. This belief completely ignores repentance, humility, and sorrow for sin and behaving like Christians. It retards Christian growth. This is how many liberal, compromising Christians get their big numbers. They try t make everyone feel comfortable in their sin and then they brag about their big numbers that they claim to have converted." **Mark Finkbeiner,** Richland Missionary Baptist Church

"One day I watched one of those trainees talk to a teenage fellow. As I listened it was evident the teenager did not understand what he was doing and did not get saved. Yet when the counselor was done, the young man believed that he was saved. That high school student had no conviction of sin; no conception of Christ's dying in his place to pay for his sin, no comprehension of trusting in Christ alone for salvation. Rather, just about all he got was that he was to bow his head and ask Jesus into his heart... That day, I doubted. I doubted that asking Jesus to come into your heart was valid. That provoked me to study. Since then I have come to the conclusion that the Bible does not teach that a person gets saved by asking Jesus Christ to come into his heart or into his life." **G. Michael Cocoris, in** *Evangelism- A Biblical Approach*

"Decisionism is the belief that a person is saved by coming forward, raising the hand, saying a prayer, believing a doctrine, making a lordship commitment, or some other external, human act, which is taken as the equivalent to, and proof of, the miracle of inward conversion... Decionism is purely human, carnal, and natural. Conversion is from God. Decisionism is from man. In Decisionism a person does something which takes the place of a saving encounter with Jesus but is, in fact, not that at all. That is why so many people are unsaved today." **R.L. Hymers, Jr. and Christopher Cagan**, *in Today's Apostasy*

"The way of salvation is falsely defined. In most instances the modern 'evangelist' assures his congregation that all any sinner has to do in order to escape hell and make sure of heaven is to 'receive Christ as his personal Savior.' But such teaching is utterly misleading. No one can receive Christ as his Savior while he rejects Him as Lord! It is true, the preacher adds, that the one who accepts Christ should also surrender to Him as Lord, but he at once spoils it by asserting that through the convert fails to do so, nevertheless heaven is sure to him. That is one of the devil's lies! Those preachers who tell sinners that they may be saved without forsaking their idols, without repenting, without surrendering to the Lordship of Christ, are as erroneous and dangerous as others who insist that salvation is by works, and that heaven must be earned by our own efforts." **Arthur Pink**, *in Present Day Evangelism*

Why would churches intentionally teach the idea? It is just another way for a church organization to gain followers and believers. Some people with little faith in themselves would surely be attracted to and find comfort within a church that's ideas of being a Christian is as simple as recited words. Why try to live a Christian life if you are guaranteed a spot in Heaven? They are fooling themselves in their morality and their faith in God.

As a high school senior, I myself was influences by the idea of being *born again*. A friend of mine that I drove to school with everyday was *born again*, and he was always telling me about his faith and how his life was changed. As a youth I never gave it much thought, almost just laugh it off, and I was Christian about to get confirmed. I knew at the time I was not true to my faith, just going through the steps I was expected to do. And I never felt as though I was touch by God or Jesus for that matter. I convinced myself that I needed to be born again. One morning while driving to school I told my friend that I wanted to be *born again*. He was genuinely happy to hear me say that. He even had me recited a prayer and ask Jesus to save me. After the prayer he said, *"Now you're saved."* I can remember thinking, *"wow that was easy."* I actually felt somewhat different, like everything is going to be just fine. By the end of the day I realized that I was not any different, I did not really change my views, and I was no more connected with God or Jesus than before. I started to think about my friend's words and how I became convinced in simple words. I was almost embarrassed to think that I fell for something as silly as recited words to save me and my faith. Throughout the years I have seen more and more go through the same situation and still not changed. It is now that I came to the true understanding of what it means to accept Jesus.

Another and even more embellished teaching is that if you accept Jesus on your deathbed you will go to Heaven. The idea, known by some as *"deathbed conversion,"* was made popular from the crucifixion story in which Jesus is executed with a thief on either side.

Luke 23: 39-43, *"And one of the malefactors which were hanged railed on him, saying, If thou be Christ, save thyself and us. But the other answering rebuked him, saying dost not thou fear God, seeing thou art in the same condemnation? And we indeed justly; for we received the due reward of our* *deeds: but this man hath done nothing amiss. And he said unto Jesus, Lord; remember me when thou comest into thy kingdom. And Jesus said unto him, Verily I say unto thee, today shalt thou be with me in paradise."*

In no other gospel do we find this story. Not even in Matthew or John, whom many believe knew Jesus, do we see any reference to a conversation between Jesus and the two thieves. The conversation was probably added later to emphasize Jesus' love and care for others while showing both remorse and forgiveness. The story itself conflicts with the whole crucifixion story. Jesus rose to His father three days after His death, which was the whole plan from the beginning. He tells the remorseful thief, *"Today you shall be with me in paradise,"* indicating He will go to Heaven that night. The concept itself is mocked by non-believers who view the teaching as a comfort faith. That is; one is comforted by the thought of life after death. How can one imagine that while living an unmoral, sinful life; that he is easily forgiven by simply accepting Jesus at the very last minute with meaningless words. It is impossible for someone to truly, in their heart, mean their words and believe in Jesus out of fear and death. Some church pastors believe in it so deeply that they will administer last rights to someone who has requested it. They assure the person just before they die, *"accept Jesus as your Lord and savior and all your sins would be forgiven"*. Why even try to live as a Christian if it is that simple?

Predestination

Predestination is a religious concept, which involves the relationship between God and God's creation. Those who believe in predestination, such as John Calvin, believe that, before the Creation, God determined the fate of the universe throughout all of time and space. Predestination is the foreordaining or foreknowledge of all that will happen; with regard to the salvation of some and not others. It has been particularly associated with the teachings of St. Augustine of Hippo and John Calvin. Within Christendom, there is considerable disagreement about

God's role in setting ultimate destinies in people's life. Christians who follow the teaching generally accept that God alone decides the eternal destinations of each person without regard to man's choices, so that their future actions or beliefs follow according to God's choice. A contrasting Christian view maintains that God is completely sovereign over all things but that he chose to give each individual free will, which each person can exercise to accept or reject God's offer of salvation and hence God allows man's choice to determine his future. The view on predestination is broad on the Christian front and covers many different sides on the subject. The different divisions of the faith have in time added to and broaden the understanding to accommodate the changing beliefs of each faith, leading to many different views and some confusion. Some of the various views on Christian predestination are as follows; Conditional predestination, Temporal predestination, Single predestination, Double predestination, Infralapsarianism, Supralapsarianism and Open theism.

Like most Christian belief followers defend the notion getting inspiration from Biblical scriptures. A quote from John Calvin reads,

> *"Scripture is the school of the Holy Spirit, in which, as nothing is omitted that is both necessary and useful to know, so nothing is taught but what is expedient to know. Therefore we must guard against depriving believers of anything disclosed about predestination in Scripture, lest we seem either wickedly to defraud them of the blessing of their God or to accuse and scoff at the Holy Spirit for having published what is in any way profitable to suppress... But for those who are so cautious or fearful that they desire to bury predestination in order not to disturb weak souls - with what color will they cloak their arrogance when they accuse God indirectly of stupid thoughtlessness as if he had not foreseen the peril that they feel they have wisely met? Whoever, then, heaps odium upon the doctrine*

of predestination openly reproaches God, as if he had unadvisedly let slip something hurtful to the Church." **John Calvin, Institutes of the Christian Religion, Book III, Ch. XXI, Sec. 3, 4.**

"Predestination we call the eternal decree of God, by which He has determined in Himself, what He would have to become of every individual of mankind. For they are not all created with a similar destiny; but eternal life is foreordained for some and eternal death for others. Every man, therefore, being created for one or the other of these ends, we say he is predestinated either to life or to death," **John Calvin, Institutes of the Christian Religion, Book III, Ch. XXI, Sec. 5.**

Here are some confessional statements on predestination. The **Belgic Confession of Faith (1561)** states:

"We believe that all the posterity of Adam, being thus fallen into perdition and ruin by the sin of our first parents, God then did manifest himself such as he is; that is to say, merciful and just: Merciful, since he delivers and preserves from this perdition all whom he, in his eternal and unchangeable council, of mere goodness hath elected in Christ Jesus our Lord, without respect to their works: Just, in leaving others in the fall and perdition wherein they have involved themselves."

The **Westminster Confession of Faith (1643)** states:

"God from all eternity did by the most wise and holy counsel of his own will, freely and unchangeably ordain whatsoever comes to pass; yet so as thereby neither is God

the author of sin; nor is violence offered to the will of the creatures, nor is the liberty or contingency of second causes taken away, but rather established. By the decree of God, for the manifestation of his glory, some men and angels are predestinated unto everlasting life, and others foreordained to everlasting death. As God hath appointed the elect unto glory, so hath He, by the eternal and most free purpose of His will, foreordained all the means thereunto. Wherefore, they who are elected . . . are effectually called unto faith in Christ by His Spirit working in due season, are justified, adopted, sanctified, and kept by His power. Through faith, unto salvation. Neither are any other redeemed by Christ, effectually called, justified, adopted, sanctified, and saved, but the elect only. The rest of mankind God was pleased, according to the unsearchable counsel of His own will, whereby He extendeth or withholdeth mercy, as He pleaseth, for the glory of His Sovereign power over His creatures, to pass by; and to ordain them to dishonor and wrath for their sin, to the praise of His glorious justice."
(Chap. III — Articles I, III, VI and VII)

The Roman Catholic Church calls predestination *God's Plan* and states that this plan also includes free will for mankind. **Catechism of the Catholic Church #600** says:

"To God, all moments of time are present in their immediacy. When therefore he establishes his eternal plan of 'predestination', he includes in it each person's free response to his grace: 'In this city, in fact, both Herod and Pontius Pilate, with the Gentiles and the peoples of Israel, gathered together against your holy servant Jesus, whom you anointed, to do whatever your hand and your plan had predestined to take place.' **(Acts 4:27-28; cf. Ps 2:1-2)**

For the sake of accomplishing his plan of salvation, God permitted the acts that flowed from their blindness." **(cf. Mt 26:54; Jn 18:36; 19:11; Acts 3:17-18)**

The idea of predestination and *free will* being tied together has a more appealing stance than predestination on its own. Predestination does not account for why horrible things happen to people by other people. Surely God did not plan on someone killing someone else. Surely his plan was not for some innocent person or child to be afflicted by the brutal acts of another. Maybe predestination is only valid when one's decision was based on God's plan. That is, when we are exposed to a situation in which we have to decide we make the decision that would be right with God. If someone makes the wrong decision in a situation and that decision leads to unexpected consequence like the death or disability of another, then would that not be the act of one's *freewill?* That decision of course is not being right with God, and God not interfering with *free will* would explain why bad things happen to good people. So in order for predestination to be Biblically valid and accepted then everyone will have to make the right decision at all times and in every situation. This, reasonably speaking, will never be the case and the reason why predestination will always be debated.

Jesus died on Wednesday

Not as much of a false teaching as a miss-understanding. But the practice of *Good Friday* has never nor will ever change. As discussed in the previous chapter under *"History of Easter"* traditional belief is that Jesus died on Good Friday, the day before the weekly Sabbath which is Saturday. Most Christians can read all four of the gospels and never catch the reference of the two Sabbaths in the week Jesus died. The gospels seem to be written in a code form, in which only a careful reader can interpret. In order to get the whole picture you must read each book carefully, observe and pick out the content as they compare to each other.

The events played out during the annual Passover celebration. The modern Jewish Passover and Feast of Unleavened Bread is seven days, starting with the sunset at the beginning of Nisan 15, now also called Passover. Judaism reckons the beginning of each day at sunset, not at midnight as in Western reckoning. Nisan 14 was commonly called Passover, technically it is the Preparation Day for the seven-day Feast of Unleavened Bread. We know that Jesus died on Wednesday, (Nisan 14) before the Passover feast on Thursday, (Nisan 15.) The Passover feast was the annual Sabbath. All traditions of the weekly Sabbath applied as well to the annual Sabbath including not working. In the third book of Moses called Leviticus there is a guidebook on how to worship, serve, and obey a holy God.

Leviticus 23:5-7, *"In the fourteenth day of the first month at even is the Lord's Passover. And on the fifteenth day of same month is the feast of unleavened bread unto the Lord: seven days ye must eat unleavened bread. In the first day ye shall have an holy convocation: ye shall do no servile work therein."*

The day Jesus died His body had to be removed because no dead body could remain on the cross due to the laws of the Sabbath.

John 19:31, *"The Jews therefore, because it was the preparation, that the bodies should not remain upon the cross on the Sabbath day, (for that Sabbath was a high day."*

Verse 42, *"There laid they Jesus therefore because of the Jews' preparation day."*

We know the preparation day was the Wednesday, (Nisan 14) before the annual Sabbath. Such an important event they had to prepare the day before because no work could be done during the Sabbath. In Mark's gospel he clearly states the Jews preparing for Passover.

Mark 15:42, *"And now when the even was come, because it was the preparation, that is, the day before the Sabbath."*

The Jews by tradition rested on the Passover, (Nisan 15). We also know about a conversation between Pilate and the Pharisees on the Passover.

Matthew 27:62, *"Now the next day, that followed the day of the preparation, the chief priest and Pharisees came together unto Pilate."*

The next day was Thursday (Nisan 15).

Mark 16:1, *"And when the Sabbath was past, Mary Magdalene, and Mary the mother of James, and Salome, had bought sweet spices, that they might come and anoint him."* Friday, (Nisan 16)

That Friday was the only day they could do any work preparation on Jesus' body for His resurrection. Because of the next Sabbath, Saturday (Nisan 17) they too had to rest to uphold Jewish Law.

Luke 23:56, *"And they returned, and prepared spices and ointments (Friday Nisan 16); and rested the Sabbath day (Saturday Nisan 17) according to the commandments."*

Jesus was resurrected that Sunday, (Nisan 18) or more likely the day before. **Mark 16:2,**

"And very early in the morning the first day of the week, they came unto the sepulcher at the rising sun."

If you read **Luke 23:53-24:1** carefully you will see the week's events unfolding.

"And he took it down, and wrapped it in linen, and it in a sepulcher that was hewn in stone. Wherein never man before was laid. And that day,

(Nisan 14) *was the preparation, and the Sabbath drew on,* (Nisan 15.) *And the women also, which came with him from Galilee, followed after, and beheld the sepulcher, and how his body was laid. And they returned,* (Nisan 16) *and prepared spices and ointments; and rested the Sabbath day,* (Nisan 17) *according to the commandments. Now upon the first day of the week,* (Nisan 18) *very early in the morning, they came unto the sepulcher, bringing the spices which they prepare."*

If Jesus had died on Friday, (Nisan 16) then there would have only been a day and a half between His death and the resurrection. In order for Him to be the true Messiah and fulfill prophesy there must be three days between.

Mark 10:34, *"And the third day He shall rise again."*

Luke 18:33, *"And they shall scourge him, and put him to death: and the third day he shall rise again."*

Anything less than three days and He would have been perceived as a false prophet. All faith in His divinity would have been lost and His disciples would have been also.

Why do Christians affiliate Friday as the day in which Jesus died? It all started from the original Greek language. Somewhere throughout the translations the tense of a critical word changed. Look at **Matthew 28:1,**

"In the end of the Sabbath, as it began to dawn toward the first day of the week."

It should have been translated to *Sabbaths* indicating that two Sabbaths had passed.

Matthew 28:1 (MGNT), ὀψὲ δὲ σαββάτων τῇ ἐπιφωσκούσῃ εἰς μίαν σαββάτων ἦλθεν Μαριὰμ ἡ Μαγδαληνὴ καὶ ἡ ἄλλη Μαρία θεωρῆσαι τὸν τάφον

The Greek word sabbatwn (sabbaton) in original Greek means Sabbaths, plural form. Over time the word has been rendered to its singular form, Sabbath. Since it has been translated incorrectly as Sunday or *"first day of the week"* a Bible reader inadvertently acknowledges only one Sabbath. Original Greek does not say *"the first day of the week,"* the original Greek is *mia twn sabbatwn,""mia ton sabbaton,"* which means*"First of Sabbaths."* This expression, which has been incorrectly translated as *"Sunday"* or *"the first day of the week,"* actually refers to the wave sheaf offering. The wave sheaf offering was a yearly offering made to God from the first grains of the harvest and it always falls on the first Sunday after Passover, what we refer to as Easter Sunday.

In defense to celebrating on Nisan 14 Polycrates of Ephesus emphatically notes that he was following the tradition passed down to him.

> *"As for us, then, we scrupulously observe the exact day, neither adding nor taking away. For in Asia great luminaries have gone to their rest who will rise again on the day of the coming of the Lord.... These all kept the 14th day of the month as the beginning of the Paschal feast, in accordance with the Gospel.... Seven of my relatives were bishops, and I am the eighth, and my relatives always observed the day when the people put away the leaven."* **Church History, Eusebius p. 5.24.**

Peter, bishop of Alexandria also defends that date,

> *"On the fourteenth day of the month, being accurately observed after the equinox, the ancients celebrate the Passover, according to the divine command."* **Chronicon Paschale**

By interpreting the Bible wrong it has been believed that Jesus died on Friday, which is why it is practice to this day as *Good Friday.*

Eventually this has been accepted by the church and yet the tradition continues to be the same. Even with undisputed historical evidence that there were indeed two Sabbaths some will not admit to error in fear of doubting their faith. The majority of all Christians will still practice and believe the events not knowing any different.

Martin Luther (Protestant Reformation)

On Halloween day 1517, a ninety-five page thesis was nailed to the Wittenberg Church door. This thesis accused the Roman Catholic Church of heresy and challenged the church's position on individual salvation. Behind the thesis was a Christian theologian and Augustine monk named Martin Luther (November 10, 1483-Februray 18, 1546). Martin Luther believed, after years of studying scriptures, that the scriptures in the Bible were telling him more than what the Roman Catholic Church was preaching. He believed the church was holding back certain church truth regarding the Bible and had lost sight of the true meaning of being Christian. Luther disagreed with the church position or repentance of sin and believed that salvation was a gift from God for those who prayed. He felt that you do not have to confess your sins to a priest, but believed in God's promise to forgive sins.

In 1520 Luther's Protestant views were condemned as Heretical by Pope Leo X. On April 7, 1521 he was summoned to renounce or reaffirm his views during the Diet of Worms. Refusing to denounce his own teaching the Emperor issued the Edit of Worms declaring Luther an outlaw of the Church.

In September of 1522 he first published the *Luther German New Testament Translation*. The foundation of his work was a 1516 Greek copy of *Erasmus*, later *called textus receptus*. By 1534 he completely translated the entire Bible in the German language. He also wrote several hymns which spawned the tradition of the congregation singing during church services.

The Protestant Reformation was the first branch to develop from the Christian tree. Martin Luther took with him the values and ideas he believed the church should stand for. Since then church leaders have followed his example and have also made the decision to branch off into new ideas and belief. Just as a tree branch is unique in form and goes into different directions so does the Christian faith. From the time of the original church, Roman Catholic and Eastern Orthodox, to the Protestant Reformation was a span of fifteen hundred years. Since then well over one hundred and forty branches have developed, each unique in its own.

Faith around Scriptures

One such belief started by George Went Hensly of eastern Tennessee around 1910 involves the handling of poisonous rattle snakes. The belief is based around the scriptures of **Mark 16:17-18,**

"And these signs shall follow them that believed; in my name shall that cast out devils; they shall speak with new tonques; They shall take up serpents; and if they drink any deadly thing, it shall not hurt them; they shall lay hand on the sick, and they shall recover."

Members of the Holiness Pentecostal faith are religious fundamentalist who believe the Bible is to be taken literally. Scattered about the Appalachian mountain in rural churches are about two thousand followers of the faith. Snake handlers only make up about 10% of the congregation.

It would be an impressive sign of devotion to see people high on faith singing dancing, speaking in tongues and picking up rattle snakes for all to see. They have taken the verse more literally and started to incorporate drinking cyanide poison. They start with small doses to build their body immune to the poison. Then they are then able to take a dose that would kill an average man and live. It is almost a con to see them drink the poison knowing they are immune from it.

Some members have died from being bitten, when this happen; the followers say that it was God's will for them to die. They do not consider the fact that the person decided to attend the service and the person made the decision to pick up the snakes. It has been estimated that around eighty people have died from snake bites since the faith started in the early 1900's. The followers seem to be unable to separate mans will from God's will.

Jehovah's Witness are another organization that interprets Bible scriptures to their will. Not so much the followers but the founders. They were founded in 1876, as the Bible study movement by Charles Taze Russell. On July 26, 1931 the name Jehovah's Witnesses was adopted. The name arose from a combination of Bible scriptures and translations from ancient Hebrew text. In the 7th-11th century the Masoretic Text vocalized the Hebrew term יהוה as הַ.וֹ.הִי (YeHoWah/JeHoVaH). The Bible was first published in English by John Wycliffe in 1382 A.D. In 1534 A.D., William Tyndale was the first to introduce the name Jehovah in its English form. There was much debate about the correct pronunciation of the name because there was no true transaltion of the Hebrew word YHWH pronounced as Yod, He, Waw, He. The Tetragrammaton is translated as Yahweh and is the true name of God. Jehovah's Witnesses defend their name because of its scripture origin.

Exodus 6:3, *"And I appeared unto Abraham, unto Isaac, and unto Jacob, by the name of God almighty, but by my name Jehovah was I not known to them."* **Isaiah 43:10,** *"Ye are my witnesses, saith the Lord, and the servenats whom I have chosen."*

Acts 10:41, *"Not to all the people, but unto witnesses chosen before of God."*

Jehovah's Witnesses feel they are the chosen people and the only people who are truly saved. Verse upon verse within the Bible speaks to them about witnessing.

John 5:31-32, *"If I bear witness of myself, my witness is not true. There is another that beareth witness of me; and I know that the witness which he witnesseth of me is true."*

Acts 22:15, *"For thou shalt be his witness unto all men of what thou hast seen and heard."*

Matthew 24:14, *"And this gospel of the kingdom shall be preached in all the world for a witness unto all nations."*

The idea of witnessing is such an important aspect of Jehovah's Witnesses, that they go door-to-door on their mission distributing literature such as *The Watchtower* and *Awake.* One of their famous preaching is the idea that only 144,000 humans will go to heaven while the rest live on an earthly paradise. This idea is also from scripture.

Revelation 14:1-3, *"And I looked, and, lo, a Lamb stood on the Mount Sion, and with him an hundred forty and four thousand, having his father's name written in their foreheads."*

Using scripture to build belief has gained the Jehovah's Witnesses over 7.1 million members around the world. They accept the Bible as scientifically and historically accurate as well as reliable enough to interpret it literally. In doing so they developed their own Bible called New World Translation. In the KJV Bible *Lord* appears 6749 times. Within their version, NWT, they replaced *Lord,* (when reference is to God not Jesus) each time with *Jehovah.* They renamed *the Old Testament* as *Hebrew-Aramaic Scriptures* and *the New Testament* as the *Christian Greek Scriptures .*It is important to mention that there is no evidence of YHWW in any of the 5000 discovered copies of Greek scriptures. It is only a Hebrew translation of God and therefore the translation should not be found in their *Christian Greek Scriptures.* They continue to modernize the Bible to make it easier for members to read and to fit their belief. In doing so the verse underwent changes from the original meaning.

Numbers 34:1, *"And the Lord spake unto Moses, saying."*

Number 34:1 (NWT), *"And Jehovah spoke further to Moses, saying."*

Jeremiah 10:1, *"Hear ye the word which the Lord speaketh unto you, O house of Israel."*

And **Jeremiah 10:1 (NWT)**, *"Hear the word that Jehovah has spoken against YOU people, O House of Israel."*

Followers of Jehovah's Witness are forbidden to read religious material not approved by The Watch Tower. Therefore many members are not aware of the belief they are practicing and how their founders intentional miss-translated the Bible. Just like the Catholic faith the members are only to know and learn what the church is to teach, and they are not to be questioned.

The Disciples of Christ are another example of a church build upon scriptures. They originally were part of Church of Christ but disagreement upon views and ideas lead them apart. The term *disciple* is derived from the New Testament Greek word "μαθητής", translated to English from the Latin word *discipulus* meaning *"a learner."* Disciples are followers or students of Jesus. The idea of being a Disciple of Christ is that we should be followers of the teachings of Jesus. Those that attend service are students of Jesus doing what He commanded us to do, *"make disciples of men."*

Matthew 21:6, *"And the disciples went, and did as Jesus commanded them."*

John 8:31, *"If ye continue in my word, then are ye my disciples indeed."*

In the book of Acts the word Christian first appear describing the disciples.

Acts 11:26, *"And the disciples were first called Christians in Antioch."*

Paul makes it clear in his letter that the infamous word Christians would forever reference to the followers of Jesus. The Bible tells us that after Jesus died the number of disciples increased as new followers joined the movement.

Acts 1:15, *"And in those days Peter stood up in the midst of the disciples, and said, (the number of names together were about an hundred and twenty.)*

Acts 6:1, *"And in those days, when the number of the disciples was multiplied."*

Acts 6:7, *"And the word of God increased; and the number of the disciples multiplied in Jerusalem greatly."*

It appears that to be disciples was the plan of Jesus from the start. As the years went buy more and more disciples would follow. To be Christian you are a disciple of Jesus by default. Currently the Disciples of Christ make up only a small portion of the Christian faith.

The last one hundred years has produced more divisions of Christianity than the first two thousand years. Just like Martin Luther, George Hensly, and Charles Russell, many more church leaders would follow. The current status of the Christian faith is structured around a central belief in both Jesus and God. The problem that continues to arise is that on the content and meaning of His message. Church leaders cannot fully agree or come to a census regarding what should be practiced. The outcome is more splits and divisions of faith. If the Christian faith moves forward in this same direction eventually the message will be lost forever.

At a recent church function on Thanksgiving Day 2009, I was able to be part of a community drive to feed the needy. It was comical to see several branches of the Christian faith who could not agree on something as simple as making a hot plate of food. There was arguing about food and table placement at a time in which we all should have been prepared to work together. In today's society I fear for our faith, God Bless.

Conclusion

"God is not the author of confusion"
1 Corinthians 14:33

C hristianity, the largest organized religion to date, consists of more than 2.1 billion followers, or about 32% of the world's population. The number has had a steady decline in the past two years. At the same time the total number of non-religious and atheists has declined also to about 77 million, or about 9% (atheists) of the world's population. With the number of non-religious followers dropping this is a clear sign of more people accepting religion. The numbers show that not all atheists are turning toward Christianity nor are most ex-Christians turning toward non-religious faith. What is going on? While some Christians have lost their faith and turn toward atheism, others just choose another faith. Young Christians are drilled with the importance of Jesus and church so much that some rebel against their parents and intentionally do what they know their parents would be against. Some children are unfortunate enough to be raised in an atheist household. Atheist openly rebel against religion and expose young children to this mentality of denying the existence of a deity. While these children do not understand, because they were never thought, they too rebel because religion is something they were told they could not be part of.

In 2007, a study by the Barna Group has concluded that more Christians under the age of thirty have become more critical of their faith than those of just a decade ago. The most common attributes perceived of Christians by Christians are that they are judgmental, hypocritical, old fashion and too involved in politics. Most Christians under thirty fully agree that Christianity has changed from Jesus' master plan and the faith does not look like Jesus in today's society. They found that 91% of non-Christians and 80% of Christians believe that Christianity has become anti-homosexual. Gay and lesbian relationships are on the rise and media attention toward their cause has brought them unwanted attention. With the Orthodox Church who views homosexuality as a sin, the perception is that all Christians are in agreement. With recent events in the media such as; gay marriages, abortion disputes, prayer in schools and pedophiles within the Catholic Church some Christians have been revolted by what they have seen. Christians seem to be embarrassed or ashamed of their belief because of the negative media. Combine that with the lack of faith in church leaders such as Evangelist, who preach the rapture, repentance of sin and hellfire as scare tactics, more Christians have felt the need to look elsewhere for spirituality.

As the American population slowly moves away from Christianity the largest group gaining followers are the agnostics and atheists. The search for acceptance and spirituality has lead more young people, with some form of faith left, toward New Age Spirituality. This New Age movement consists of free-flowing spiritually religious groups. Within these groups you will find no religious texts, central organization, no required membership, no formal clergy dogma or creeds. There are no forced ideas or pressured beliefs. Just a group of followers whose shared belief leads them to spiritual development they could not find anywhere.

> *"In turbulent times, in times of great changed, people head for the two extremes: fundamentalism and personal, spiritual experience… With no membership lists or even a coherent philosophy or dogma, it is difficult to define or measure the unorganized New Age movement. But in every major U.S. and European city, thousands who seek insight and personal growth cluster around a metaphysical bookstore, a spiritual teacher, or an education center."*
> **John Naisbitt**

Roughly 20% of the population represents the New Age philosophy. The New Age teaching roots are traceable to old world religions such as; Astrology, Hinduism, Buddhism, Gnostics, Toaism, Wicca, Druids, Zoroastrians, Kabbala and other neo-pagan faiths. They incorporate new ideas and beliefs with ancient traditions and festivals. They demonstrate a sense of unity and oneness to converts looking for something new that is not related to organize religion. To the younger rebellious generation the idea of belonging to a pagan religion is appealing. They view Wicca and Druids as a cool thing, only practicing it for attention not because that is who they truly are.

The following is a list from www.religioustolerance.com explaining some New Age Beliefs. Individuals of the New Age Movement are encouraged to try different belief until they find one they become comfortable with.

Monism: All that exists is derived from a single source of divine energy.

Pantheism: All that exists is God; God is all that exists. This leads naturally to the concept of the divinity of the individual, that we are all Gods. They do not seek God as revealed in a sacred text or as exists in a remote heaven; they seek God within the self and throughout the entire universe.

Panentheism: God is all that exists. God is at once the entire universe, and transcends the universe as well.

Reincarnation: After death, we are reborn and live another life as a human. This cycle repeats itself many times. This belief is similar to the concept of transmigration of the soul in Hinduism.

Karma: The good and bad deeds that we do add and subtracts from our accumulated record, our **karma**. At the end of our life, we are rewarded or punished according to our karma by being reincarnated into either a painful or good new life. This belief is linked to that of reincarnation and is also derived from Hinduism

An **Aura** is believed to be an energy field radiated by the body. Invisible to most people, it can be detected by some as a shimmering, multi-colored field surrounding the body. Those skilled in detecting and interpreting auras can diagnose an individual's state of mind, and their spiritual and physical health.

Personal Transformation: A profoundly intense mystical experience will lead to the acceptance and use of New Age beliefs and practices. Guided imagery, hypnosis, meditation, and (sometimes) the use of hallucinogenic drugs are useful to bring about and enhance this transformation. Believers hope to develop new potentials within themselves: the ability to heal oneself and others, psychic powers, a new understanding of the workings of the universe, etc. Later, when sufficient numbers of people have achieved these powers, a major spiritual, physical, psychological and cultural planet-wide transformation is expected.

Ecological Responsibility: A belief in the importance of uniting to preserve the health of the earth, which is often, looked upon as **Gaia**, (Mother Earth) a living entity.

Universal Religion: Since all is God, then only one reality exists, and all religions are simply different paths to that ultimate reality. The universal religion can be visualized as a mountain, with many **sadhanas** (spiritual paths) to the summit. Some are hard; others easy. There is no one correct path. All paths eventually reach the top. They anticipate that a new universal religion which contains elements of all current faiths will evolve and become generally accepted worldwide.

New World Order As the **Age of Aquarius** unfolds, a **New Age** will develop. This will be a utopia in which there is world government, and end to wars, disease, hunger, pollution, and poverty. Gender, racial, religious and other forms of discrimination will cease. People's allegiance to their tribe or nation will be replaced by a concern for the entire world and its people.

New Age Practices:

Channeling-A method similar to that used by Spiritists in which a spirit of a long dead individual is conjured up. However, while Spiritists generally believe that one's soul remains relatively unchanged after death, most channelers believe that the soul evolves to higher planes of existence. Channelers usually try to make contact with a single, spiritually evolved being. That being's consciousness is channeled through the medium and relays guidance and information to the group, through the use of the medium's voice. Channeling has existed since the 1850's and many groups consider themselves independent of the New Age movement. Perhaps the most famous channeling event is the popular *A Course in Miracles*. It was channeled through a Columbia University psychologist, Dr. Helen Schucman, (1909-1981), over an 8 year period. She was an Atheist, and in no way regarded herself as a New Age believer. However, she took great care in recording accurately the words that she received.

Crystals-Crystals are materials which have their molecules arranged in a specific, highly ordered internal pattern. This pattern is reflected in the crystal's external structure which typically has symmetrical planar surfaces. Many common substances, from salt to sugar, from diamonds to quartz form crystals. They can be shaped so that they will vibrate at a specific frequency and are widely used in radio communications and computing devices. New Agers believe that crystals possess healing energy.

Meditating-A process of blanking out the mind and releasing oneself from conscious thinking. This is often aided by repetitive chanting of a mantra, or focusing on an object.

New Age Music-A gentle, melodic, inspirational music form involving the human voice, harp, lute, flute, etc. It is used as an aid in healing, massage therapy and general relaxation.

Divination-The use of various techniques to foretell the future, including I Ching, Pendulum movements, Runes, Scrying, Tarot Cards.

Astrology-The belief that the orientation of the planets at the time of one's birth and the location of that birth predicts the individual's future and personality. Belief in astrology is common amongst New Agers, but definitely not limited to them.

Holistic Health- This is a collection of healing techniques which have diverged from the traditional medical model. It attempts to cure disorders in mind, body and spirit and to promote wholeness and balance in the individual. Examples are acupuncture, crystal healing, homeopathy, iridology, massage, various meditation methods, polarity therapy, psychic healing, therapeutic touch, reflexology, etc.

Human Potential Movement (a.k.a. Emotional Growth Movement)-This is a collection of therapeutic methods involving both individualized and group working, using both mental and physical techniques. The goal is to help individuals to advance spiritually. Examples are Esalen Growth Center programs, EST, Gestalt Therapy, Primal Scream Therapy, Transactional Analysis, Transcendental Meditation and Yoga.

All text is from http://www.religioustolerance.org/newage.html

The fate of Christianity resides in the hands of the infants and children of today. In order for the faith to move back toward the message of Jesus, the generation to come must be properly educated on the truth regarding Christianity. All the history is important from the good to the bad to the ugly. Only then could the proper picture be exposed and the right mind set is developed to appreciate the faith as it should be. Churches have always been open to the public for those seeking religious guidance. They now need to open up to each other. They have to accept their difference and work together to bring unity and oneness to a split faith. Only then can the fate of Christianity be protected and secure for the next generation.

Ecumenical Councils

An ecumenical council is a legal assembly of ecclesiastical dignitaries and theological experts of the whole Christian Church that convened to discuss and settle matters of Church doctrine, discipline and practice. *Ecumenical* derives from a Greek word which literally means *"the inhabited world"* which first referred to the Roman Empire and was later extended to apply to the world in general.

Church councils were, from the beginning, bureaucratic exercises. Written documents were circulated, speeches were made and responded to, votes were taken, and final documents published then distributed. A large part of what we know about the beliefs of heresies comes from the documents quoted in councils in order to be refuted.

Most councils dealt with both doctrinal and disciplinary matters, which were decided in laws called *"canons"*. Canons consist of doctrinal statements and disciplinary measures. Most Church councils dealt with immediate disciplinary concerns as well as major difficulties of doctrine. Eastern Orthodoxy typically views the purely doctrinal canons as dogmatic and applicable to the entire church at all times, while the disciplinary canons apply to a particular time and place and may or may not be applicable in other situations.

Apostolic Council

49 A.D. St. Paul assembled several apostles in Jerusalem. They were to determine how gentiles would be admitted into the Church. This can be read in **Acts 15:1-29.**

Early Councils

325 A.D. *Council of Nicaea* lasted from May 20,325-July 25, 325 A.D. Three hundred and eighteen bishops were present. Hosius, Bishop of Cordova, assisted as legate of Pope Sylvester. The Emperor Constantine was also present, but made no decision on church dogma. To this council we owe *The Nicene Creed,* defining against Arius the true Divinity of the Son of God, and fixing the date of Easter.

363-364 A.D. *Council of Laodicea* was a regional synod of approximately thirty clerics from Asia Minor, that assembled about 363-364 A.D. in Laodicea, Phrygia Pacatiana. The major concerns of the Council involved constricting the conduct of church members, and the canon of scriptures. They decided on the books both allowed and band to be read. The 59th canon restricted the readings in church to only the canonical books of the Old and New Testaments. The 60th canon listed these books, with the New Testament containing 26 books, omitting the Book of Revelation, and the Old Testament including the 22 books of the Hebrew Bible plus the *Book of Baruch* and the *Epistle of Jeremy.*

381 A.D. *First Council of Constantinople,* under Pope Damascus and the Emperor Theodosius I, was attended by 150 bishops. It was directed against the followers of Macedonius, who impugned the Divinity of the Holy Ghost. To the above-mentioned Nicene Creed it added the clauses referring to the Holy Ghost (*qui simul adoratur*) and all that follows to the end.

382 A.D. *Council of Rome* was a meeting of Christian Church officials and theologians which took place in 382 A.D. under the authority of the Damascus I, bishop of Rome. The previous year, the Emperor Theodosius I had appointed the *"dark horse"* candidate Nectarius Archbishop of Constantinople. Soon after the close of the First Council of Constantinople in 381 A.D., the Imperial bishops were summoned to a new council at Constantinople; nearly all of the same bishops who had attended the earlier second council were assembled again in early summer of 382 A.D.

397 A.D. *Council of Carthage* assembled under Cyprian to consider the treatment of the lapsi, excommunicated Felicissimus and five other Novatian bishops, and declared that the lapsi should be dealt with, not with indiscriminate severity, but according to the degree of individual guilt.

415 A.D. *Council of Carthage* appealed to **1 John 5:7** when debating the Arian belief, (Arians didn't believe in the deity of Jesus Christ). Prior to this council, a conflict had arisen between the Arians and a group of bishops from North Africa. An assembly was called at Carthage where **I John 5:7-8** was insisted upon by Eugenius, the spokesman for the African bishops. The bishops included the *Johannine Comma* as a first line of defense for their confession of Christ's deity. Acting as spokesman for some 350 church bishops Eusebius confessed his faith and the faith of his brethren with these words: *"and in order that we may teach until now, more clearly than light, that the Holy Spirit is now one divinity with the Father and the Son. It is proved by the evangelist John, for he says, "There are three which bear testimony in heaven, the Father, the Holy Ghost, and the Holy Spirit, and these three are one."*

431 A.D. *Council of Ephesus,* of which more than 200 bishops attended presided over by St. Cyril of Alexandria representing Pope Celestine l, defined the true personal unity of Christ, declared Mary the Mother of God against Nestorius, Bishop of Constantinople, and renewed the condemnation of Pelagius.

451 A.D. *Council of Chalcedon,* of which 150 bishops attended under Pope Leo the Great and the Emperor Marcian, defined the two natures (Divine and human) in Christ against Eutyches, who was excommunicated.

529 A.D. *The Second Council of Orange* was the result of two church councils held in Orange, France in 441 A.D. and 529 A.D. The first Council dealt with a range of administrative and practical issues in the church, including an affirmation of celibacy for priests, deacons, and widows; the right of sanctuary or asylum; the administration of sacraments; the relationship and jurisdiction of bishops; and the calling of church councils. The second Council dealt more directly with ongoing theological issues surrounding the conflict between Augustine, Bishop of Hippo in North Africa (354-430 A.D.) and Pelagius, a British monk (354 -420/440 A.D.) who challenged some of the traditional views of the Church, especially as presented by Augustine. Pelagius had denied the Augustinian doctrine of original sin, which held that human beings were so corrupted by sin they had no will to choose God.

553 A.D. *Second Council of Constantinople,* of which 165 bishops attended under Pope Vigilius and Emperor Justinian I, condemned the errors of Origen and certain writings *(The Three Chapters)* of Theodoret of Theodore, Bishop of Mopsuestia and of Ibas, Bishop of Edessa; it further confirmed the first four general councils, especially that of Chalcedon whose authority was contested by some heretics.

680 A.D. *Third Council of Constantinople,* under Pope Agatho and the Emperor Constantine Pogonatus, was attended by the Patriarchs of Constantinople and of Antioch, 174 bishops, and the emperor. It put an end to Monothelitism by defining two wills in Christ, the Divine and the human, as two distinct principles of operation.

787 A.D. *Second Council of Nicaea* was assembled by Emperor Constantine VI and his mother Irene, under Pope Adrian I, and was presided over by the legates of Pope Adrian; it regulated the veneration of holy images. Between 300 and 367 bishops assisted.

869 A.D. *Fourth Council of Constantinople,* under Pope Adrian II and Emperor Basil attending were 102 bishops, 3 papal legates, and 4 patriarchs, consigned to the flames the Acts of an irregular council brought together by Photius against Pope Nicholas and Ignatius the legitimate Patriarch of Constantinople; it condemned Photius who had unlawfully seized the patriarchal dignity. The Photian Schism, however, triumphed in the Greek Church, and no other general council took place in the East.

1123 A.D. *First Lateran Council* held at Rome under Pope Callistus II. About 900 bishops and abbots assisted. It abolished the right claimed by lay princes, and dealt with church discipline and the recovery of the Holy Land from the infidels.

1139 A.D. *Second Lateran Council* was held at Rome under Pope Innocent II with an attendance of about 1000 prelates and the Emperor Conrad. Its object was to put an end to the errors of Arnold of Brescia.

1179 A.D. *Third Lateran Council* took place under Pope Alexander III, Frederick I being emperor. There were 302 bishops present. It condemned the Albigenses and Waldenses and issued numerous decrees for the reformation of morals.

1215 A.D. *Fourth Lateran Council* took place under Innocent III. Attending were the Patriarchs of Constantinople and Jerusalem, 71 archbishops, 412 bishops, and 800 abbots the Primate of the Maronites, and St. Dominic. It issued an enlarged creed against the Albigenses, condemned the Trinitarian errors of Abbot Joachim, and published 70 important reformatory decrees.

1245 A.D. *First Council of Lyons* took place under Innocent IV. In attendance were the Patriarchs of Constantinople, Antioch, and Aquileia (Venice), 140 bishops, Baldwin II, Emperor of the East, and St. Louis, King of France. It excommunicated and deposed Emperor Frederick II and directed a new crusade, under the command of St. Louis, against the Saracens and Mongols.

1274 A.D. *Council of Lyons* convened with Pope Gregory X, the Patriarchs of Antioch and Constantinople, 15 cardinals, 500 bishops, and more than 1000 other dignitaries. It affected a temporary reunion of the Greek Church with Rome. The word *filioque* was added to the symbol of Constantinople and means were sought for recovering Palestine from the Turks. It also laid down the rules for papal elections.

1311 A.D. *Council of Vienne* in France was order by Clement V, the first of the Avignon popes. In attendance were the Patriarchs of Antioch and Alexandria, 300 bishops, and 3 kings Philip IV of France, Edward II of England, and James II of Aragon. The synod dealt with the crimes and errors imputed to the Knights Templars, the Fraticelli, the Beghards, and the Beguines, with projects of a new crusade, the reformation of the clergy, and the teaching of Oriental languages in the universities.

1403 A.D. *Council of Pisa* convened to attempt to solve the Great Schism of the West, but was unsuccessful. The council is *not recognized* by the Orthodox Church because it was not convened by a pope and its outcome was repudiated at Constance.

1414 A.D. *Council of Constance* was held during the Great Schism of the West, with the object of ending the divisions in the Church. It only became legitimate when Gregory XI had assembled it. Owing to this circumstance it succeeded in putting an end to the schism by the election of Pope Martin V, which the Council of Pisa (1403 A.D.) had failed to accomplish on account of its illegality. The rightful pope confirmed the former decrees of the synod against Wycliffe and Hus. This council is thus only ecumenical in its last sessions and with respect to the decrees of earlier sessions approved by Martin V.

1431 A.D. *Council of Basle* convened under Popes Martin V and Eugene IV. Its object was the religious pacification of Bohemia. Quarrels with the pope having arisen, the council was transferred first to Ferrara in 1438 A.D., then to Florence in 1439 A.D., where a short-lived union with the Greek Church was effected. The Council of Basle is only ecumenical till the end of the twenty-fifth session and of its decrees Eugene IV approved only such as dealt with the extirpation of heresy, the peace of Christendom, and the reform of the Church.

1512 A.D. *Fifth Lateran Council* convened under Popes Julius II and Leo X, the emperor being Maximilian I. Fifteen cardinals and about eighty archbishops and bishops took part in it. Its decrees are chiefly disciplinary. A new crusade against the Turks was also planned, but never materialized, because of the religious upheaval in Germany under Luther.

1545 A.D. *Council of Trent* lasted eighteen years under five popes: Paul III, Julius III, Marcellus II, Paul IV and Pius IV, and under the Emperors Charles V and Ferdinand. There were present 5 cardinal legates of the Holy See, 3 patriarchs, 33 archbishops, 235 bishops, 7 abbots, 7 generals of monastic orders, and 160 doctors of divinity. It was convoked to examine and condemn the errors promulgated by Luther and other Reformers, and to reform the discipline of the Church. Of all councils it lasted longest, issued the largest number of dogmatic and reformatory decrees, and produced the most beneficial results.

1869 A.D. *First Vatican Council* was summoned to the Vatican by Pius IX. It met on December 8, and lasted till July 18, 1870, when it was adjourned. There were present 29 generals of orders, 6 archbishop-princes, 680 archbishops and bishops, 49 cardinals, 11 patriarchs, 28 abbots. Besides important canons relating to the Faith and the constitution of the Church, he defines a doctrine concerning faith or morals to be held by the whole Church.

1962 *Second Ecumenical Council of the Vatican, or Vatican II*, was the twenty-first Ecumenical Council of the Catholic Church. It opened under Pope John XXIII on October 11, and closed under Pope Paul VI on December 8, 1965. At least four future pontiffs took part in the council's opening session: Cardinal Giovanni Battista Montini, who on succeeding Pope John XXIII took the name of Paul VI; Bishop Albino Luciani, the future Pope John Paul I; Bishop Karol Wojtyła, who became Pope John Paul II; and Father Joseph Ratzinger, present as a theological consultant, who became Pope Benedict XVI.

Appendices

⌒𝓂⌒

Who's Who

Abbot Eutyches-*Abbot Eutyches,* (375-454 A.D.), was regarded as the
founder of Eutychianism, an extreme form of the Monophysite heresy
that emphasizes the exclusive prevalence of the divinity in Christ. He
studied the Christological doctrine of the Alexandrian school under
the influence of Patriarch St. Cyril. Eutyches, in professing one nature
in Christ, reflected the Eastern monastic view of Christ and opposed
the rival Antioch school, which espoused the heterodox doctrine of
Nestorius.

Archelaus-*Archelaus,* (23 B.C. – 18 A.D.), was the ethnarch of Samaria,
Judea, and Edom from 4 B.C. to 6 A.D. He was the son of Herod the
Great and Malthace, the brother of Herod Antipas, and the half-brother
of Hero Philip I. Archelaus received the kingdom of Judea by the
last will of his father, though a previous will had bequeathed it to his
brother Antipas. He was proclaimed king by the army, but declined to
assume the title until he had submitted his claims to Caesar Augustus
in Rome. Before setting out, he ruled with the utmost cruelty sedition
of the Pharisees, slaying nearly three thousand of them. In Rome he was
opposed by Antipas and by many of the Jews, who feared his cruelty;

but in 4 B.C. Augustus allotted to him the greater part of the kingdom (Samaria, Judea, and Idumea) with the title of ethnarch until 6 A.D. when Judaea was brought under direct Roman rule.

Arius-*Arius,* (250–336 A.D.), was a Christian presbyter from Alexandria, Egypt. His teachings about the nature of the Godhead, which emphasized the Father's Divinity over the Son, and his opposition to the Athanasian or Trinitarian Christology, made him a controversial figure in the First Council of Nicaea, convened by Roman Emperor Constantine in 325 A.D. After Emperor Constantine legalized and formalized the Christianity of the time in the Roman Empire, the newly recognized Catholic Church sought to unify theology.

Athanasius of Alexandria-*Athanasius of Alexandria* (Greek: *Athanásios*) (293 – May 2, 373 A.D.), also *Athanasius the Great, Pope Athanasius I of Alexandria,* and *Athanasius the Apostolic,* was a Christian theologian, bishop of Alexandria, Church Father, and a noted Egyptian leader of the fourth century. He is best remembered for his role in the conflict with Arius and Arianism. At the First Council of Nicaea, Athanasius argued against Arius and his doctrine that Christ is of a distinct substance from the Father. Athanasius is counted as one of the four Great Doctors in the Eastern Orthodox Christian tradition and is a Doctor of the Church in the Catholic Church.

Augustine of Hippo-*Augustine of Hippo,* (Latin: *Aurelius Augustinus Hipponensis* ;), (November 13, 354 – August 28, 430 A.D.), also known as *Augustine, St. Augustine,* or *St. Austin* was Bishop of Hippo Regius. He was a Latin-speaking philosopher and theologian who lived in the Roman Africa Province. His writings were very influential in the development of Western Christianity. Augustine, a Latin Church father, is one of the most important figures in the development of Western Christianity. According to his contemporary Jerome he "established anew the ancient faith" (*conditor antiquae rursum fidei*). In his early years he was heavily influenced by Manichaeism and afterward by the Neo Platonism of Plotinus. After his conversion to Christianity and baptism in 387 A.D., Augustine developed his own approach to philosophy and theology, accommodating a variety of methods and different perspectives. He believed that the grace of Christ was indispensable to human freedom and framed the concepts of original sin.

The Barna Group-_The Barna Group_ is a firm based in Ventura, California. It consists of five divisions focusing on primary research (The Barna Research Group); communications tools (BarnaFilms); printed resources (BarnaBooks); leadership development for young people (The Josiah Corps); and church facilitation and enhancement (Transformation Church Network). It was founded in 1984 by George Barna, a media research specialist holding graduate degrees in urban planning and political science, for the purpose of providing "research and marketing expertise as a service to Christian ministry." In 1991, the company cut ties with Disney to concentrate its resources on a campaign to transform the church. According to the Barna Group, _"The ultimate aim of the firm is to partner with Christian ministries and individuals to be a catalyst in moral and spiritual transformation in the United States. It accomplishes these outcomes by providing vision, information, evaluation and resources through a network of intimate partnerships."_ Opinion polls provided by The Barna Group are frequently cited in national and international news media in articles about American religion. The concept of _notional Christians_ seems to have been created by the Barna Group for the purposes of gathering statistics. They define the term as follows: _"We categorize Notional Christian as those who describe themselves as Christians, but do not believe that they will have eternal life because of their reliance upon the death and resurrection of Jesus Christ and the grace extended to people through a relationship with Christ. (A large majority of these individuals believe they will have eternal life, but not because of a grace-based relationship with Jesus Christ.)"_ The term implies that some have the notion that they are Christian, though they do not meet the Barna Group's definition of Christian.

Caesar Augustus-*Gaius Julius Caesar Augustus,* (September 23, 63 B.C. – August 19, 14 A.D.), was the first emperor of the Roman Empire, which he ruled alone from 27 B.C. until his death in 14 A.D. In 27 B.C. the Senate awarded him the honorific *Augustus ("the revered one")*, and thus consequently he was *Gaius Julius Caesar Augustus*. Because of the various names he bore, it is common to call him *Octavius* when referring to events from 63-44 B.C., *Octavian* (or *Octavianus*) when referring to events from 44-27 B.C., and *Augustus* when referring to events after 27 B.C.

Caiaphas-*Caiaphas* Hebrew פסוי ר_ב ק.י.פ.א or *Yosef Bar Kayafa,* commonly known simply as **Caiaphas** (Greek Καϊάφας) in the New Testament, was the Roman-appointed Jewish high priest who is said to have organized the plot to kill Jesus. Caiaphas is also said to have been involved in the trial of Jesus. According to the Gospels, Caiaphas was the major antagonist of Jesus. German higher-critical scholars in the 18th and 19th centuries questioned historicity of Caiaphas. By the 20th century Jesus myth theory argued he was merely fictional character having no basis in historical fact. Then in 1990, an ornate limestone ossuary was found in the Abu Tor neighborhood of modern Jerusalem. This ossuary appeared authentic and contained human remains. The Aramaic inscription on the side which read *"Joseph son of Caiaphas."* also appeared authentic. The bones of an elder man probably belonged to the High Priest Caiaphas. This discovery is an important confirmation of a significant segment of the New Testament account of Jesus leading to a greater understanding of the historical Jesus.

Callistus-*Pope Saint Callixtus I* or *Callistus I,* was pope from about 217- 222 A.D., during the reigns of the Roman Emperors Elagabalus and Alexander Severus. He was martyred for his Christian faith and is a saint of the Roman Catholic Church.

Canaan-The Bible reveals that Canaan was the fourth son of Ham and brother of Mizraim. It was Canaan, the grandson of Noah who Noah had cursed in **Genesis 9:25**. The descendants of Canaan are listed in **Genesis 10:15-19**. The Canaanites actually became a general term for *"all the inhabitants"* of the land of ancient Israel, and especially to the tribe who dwelt west of the Dead Sea and had conquered the whole area east of the Jordan River.

Cassiodorus-*Flavius Magnus Aurelius Cassiodorus Senator* (485 – 585 A.D.), commonly known as *Cassiodorus,* was a Roman statesman and writer, serving in the administration of Theodoric the Great, king of the Ostrogoths. *Senator* was part of his surname, not his rank.

Charles Taze Russell-*Charles Taze Russell,* (February 16, 1852 – October 31, 1916), or *Pastor Russell,* was a prominent early 20th century Christian Restorationist minister from Pittsburgh, Pennsylvania, and founder of what is now known as the Bible Student movement, from which Jehovah's Witnesses and numerous independent Bible Student groups emerged. Beginning in July, 1879 he began publishing a monthly religious journal *Zion's Watch Tower and Herald of Christ's Presence.* The magazine is now published semi-monthly under the name, *The Watchtower Announcing Jehovah's Kingdom.* In 1881, he co-founded Zion's Watch Tower Tract Society and in 1884 the corporation was officially registered, with Russell as president. Russell was a prolific writer, producing many articles, books, pamphlets and sermons, totaling 50,000 printed pages, with almost 20 million copies of his books printed and distributed around the world. From 1886 to 1904, he published a six-part series entitled *The Millennial Dawn,* which later became known as *Studies in the Scriptures.*

Constantine-*Caesar Flavius Valerius Aurelius Constantinus Augustus,* (February 27, 272 – May 22, 337 A.D.), commonly known in English as *Constantine I, Constantine the Great. Saint Constantine* was Roman emperor from 306 A.D., until his death in 337 A.D. best known for being the first Christian Roman emperor, Constantine reversed the persecutions of his predecessor, Diocletian, and issued the Edict of Milan in 313 A.D., which proclaimed religious tolerance of Christians throughout the empire. The Byzantine liturgical calendar, observed by the Eastern Orthodox Church and Eastern Catholic Churches of Byzantine rite, lists both Constantine and his mother Helena as saints. Although he is not included in the Latin Church's list of saints, which does recognize several other Constantines as saints, he is revered under the title *"The Great"* for his contributions to Christianity.

Craig L. Blomberg-*Criag L. Blombeg* is the Distinguished Professor of the New Testament, and has been a New Testament scholar since 1986, at Denver Seminary in Colorado. He received his Ph.D. from University of Aberdeen, Scotland; his M.A. from Trinity Evangelical Divinity School, and completed his B.A., *Summa Cum Laude*, at Augustana College. He was an assistant professor of Religion at Palm Beach Atlantic College from 1982–85 and took a leave of absence to accept a one-year research fellowship in Cambridge, England with the British wing of the InterVarsity Christian Fellowship from 1985-86. During this time, he co-edited *Gospel Perspectives, vol. 6: The Miracle of Jesus* and wrote *The Historical Reliability of the Gospels.*

Crispus-*Flavius Julius Crispus*, also known as *Flavius Claudius Crispus* and *Flavius Valerius Crispus* was a Caesar of the Roman Empire. He was the first-born son of Constantine I and Minervina.

Cyprian of Carthage -*Saint Cyprian* Latin: *Thascius Caecilius Cyprianus* (208-September 14, 258 A.D.), was bishop of Carthage and an important early Christian writer. He was born in the beginning of the third century in North Africa, perhaps at Carthage, where he received a classical education. After converting to Christianity, he became a bishop in 249 A.D. and eventually died a martyr at Carthage.

Cyrenius-*Publius Sulpicius Quirinius* (Greek Κυρήνιος - *Kyrenios* or *Cyrenius*, (51 B.C. – 21 A.D.) was a Roman aristocrat. As governor of Syria, he carried out the famous census of Judea in 6 A.D.

Cyril of Jerusalem-*Cyril of Jerusalem* was a distinguished theologian of the early Church (313 – 386 A.D.). He is venerated as a saint by the Roman Catholic Church, the Eastern Orthodox Church, and the Anglican Communion. In 1883, Cyril was declared a Doctor of the Church by Pope Leo XIII.

Diocletianus- *Gaius Aurelius Valerius Diocletianus,* (December 22, 244 – December 3, 311 A.D.), born *Diocles* and commonly known as *Diocletian,* was Roman Emperor from November 20, 284 - 1 May 1, 305 A.D. The Diocletian Persecution (303–11 A.D.), the empire's, largest, and bloodiest persecution of Christianity, did not destroy the empire's Christian community. After 324 A.D. Christianity became the empire's preferred religion under its first Christian emperor, Constantine.

Dionysis Bishop of Rome-*Pope Saint Dionysius* was pope from July 22, 259-December 26, 268 A.D. Dionysius was elected pope in 259 A.D., after the martyrdom of Sixtus II in 258 A.D. The Holy See had been vacant for nearly a year due to difficulty in electing a new pope during the violent persecution which Christians faced. When the persecution had begun to subside, Dionysius was raised to the office of Bishop of Rome.

Dionysius Exiguus-*Dionysius Exiguus,* (470–544 A.D.) was a sixth century monk born in Scythia Minor, modern Dobruja, Romania. He was a member of the Scythian monks community concentrated in Tomis, the major city of Scythia Minor. The author of a continuation of *Dionysius's Computus,* writing in 616 A.D., described Dionysius as a *"most learned abbot of the city of Rome",* and the Venerable Bede accorded him the honorific *abbas,* which could be applied to any monk, especially a senior and respected monk, and does not necessarily imply that Dionysius ever headed a monastery. Dionysius is best-known as the inventor of the *Anno Domini era*, which is used to number the years of both the Gregorian calendar and the Julian calendar.

Emperor Aurelian-*Lucius Domitius Aurelianus,* (September 9, 214– October 275 A.D.), commonly known as *Aurelian*, was Roman Emperor from 270- 275 A.D. Aurelian restored the empire's eastern provinces after his conquest of the Palmyrene Empire in 273 A.D. The following year he conquered the Gallic Empire in the west, reuniting the empire in its entirety. He was also responsible for the construction of the Aurelian Walls in Rome, and the abandonment of the province of Dacia. His successes effectually ended the empire's Crisis of the Third Century. He is most notable for designating December twenty-fifth as the official celebration day of Mithras in 274 A.D.

Erasmus-*Desiderius Erasmus Roterodamus,* (October 28, 1466– July 12, 1536 A.D.), was sometimes known as *Desiderius Erasmus of Rotterdam*. He was a Dutch Renaissance humanist, a Catholic priest and theologian. Erasmus lived through the Reformation period and he consistently criticized some contemporary popular Christian beliefs. In relation to clerical abuses in the Church, Erasmus remained committed to reforming the Church from within. He held to the Catholic Church doctrine of *free will*, which some Protestant Reformers rejected in favor of the doctrine of *predestination*. His middle road approach disappointed and even angered many Protestants, such as Martin Luther, as well as conservative Catholics. He died in Basel in 1536 A.D. and was buried in the formerly Catholic cathedral there, recently converted to a Reformed church.

Emperor Theodosius-*Flavius Theodosius* (January 11,347 – January 17, 395 A.D.), commonly known as *Theodosius I* or *Theodosius the Great*, was Roman Emperor from 379-395 A.D. Theodosius was the last emperor of the Eastern and Western Roman Empire. He is known for making Nicene Christianity the official state religion of the Roman Empire.

Eusebius-*Eusebius of Caesarea*, (263–339 A.D.), called *Eusebius Pamphili*, became the Bishop of Caesarea in Palestine about the year 314 A.D. Eusebius, historian and polemicist is one of the more renowned Church Fathers. Both he and Pamphilus were scholars of the Biblical canon. He wrote *Demonstrations of the Gospel, Preparations for the Gospel*, and *On Discrepancies between the Gospels*, studies of the Biblical text. As *"Father of Church History"* he produced the *Ecclesiastical History, On the Life of Pamphilus*, the *Chronicle* and *On the Martyrs*.

Epiphanius of Salamis-*Epiphanius of Salamis* (310–320 – 403 A.D.) was bishop of Salamis and metropolitan of Cyprus at the end of the 4th century. He is considered a Church Father. He gained a reputation as a strong defender of orthodoxy. He is best known for composing a very large compendium of the heresies up to his own time, full of quotations that are often the only surviving fragments of suppressed texts, and for instigating, with Tychon (Bishop of Amathus), a persecution against the non-Christians living on Cyprus, and the destruction of most of their temples.

Eusebius of Nicomedia-*Eusebius of Nicomedia*, (died 341), was the man who baptized Constantine. He was a bishop of Berytus in Phoenicia, then of Nicomedia where the imperial court resided in Bithynia, and finally of Constantinople from 338 A.D. up to his death.

Fausta-*Fausta Flavia Maxima*, (289-326 A.D.), was a Roman Empress, daughter of the Roman Emperor Maximianus. Maximianus married her to Constantine I in 307 A.D. She supposedly killed herself after Constantine found that she lied about the allegation of his son trying to seduce her.

Gaius Caesar-*Gaius Julius Caesar,* (20 B.C. – 4 A.D.), most commonly known as *Gaius Caesar* or *Caius Caesar,* was the oldest son of Marcus Vipsanius Agrippa and Julia the Elder. He was born between August 14 and September 13, 20 B.C. or according to other sources in September 23, 20 B.C. with the name *Gaius Vipsanius Agrippa,* but when he was adopted by his maternal grandfather Roman Emperor Augustus, his name was changed to *Gaius Julius Caesar.*

Galerius-*Galerius,* (260 – May 311 A.D.), formally *Gaius Galerius Valerius Maximianus* was Roman Emperor from 305- 311 A.D. He served with distinction as a soldier under Emperors Aurelian and Probus. Soon after his appointment, Galerius would be dispatched to Egypt to fight the rebellious cities Busiris and Coptos.

George Went Hensley-*George Went Hensley,* (May 2, 1881- July 25, 1955), was one of the founders of the *Church of God with Signs Following,* a twentieth century snake handling movement that was centered in the southeastern United States. As a Tennessee native, Hensley contributed to the popularization of snake handling in North Carolina, Kentucky, Tennessee, and Virginia. Hensley is sometimes referred to as the *"father of contemporary serpent handling."* Hensley was purported to have been bitten over 400 times by the snakes he handled, always refusing medical treatment. On July 25, 1955, one of these bites proved fatal.

George M. Lamsa-George *M. Lamsa* (August 5, 1892 – September 22, 1975) was an Assyrian author. A native Aramaic speaker, he translated the Aramaic Peshitta (literally "straight, simple") Old and New Testaments into English. His hypothesis was that for the New Testament, the Peshitta was the original text, and the Greek version was translated from it. In support of this, he noted that Aramaic was the language of Jesus and the earliest Christians. Lamsa produced his own translation of the Bible in the form of *The Holy Bible from Ancient Eastern Manuscripts*, which is commonly called the *Lamsa Bible.*

Gregory Thaumaturgus-*Saint Gregory of Neocaesarea,* also known as *Gregory Thaumaturgus or Gregory the Wonderworker,* (213 –270 A.D.) was a Christian bishop of the 3rd century.

Hippolytus of Rome-*Hippolytus of Rome,* (170– 236 A.D.), was the most important third century theologian in the Christian Church in Rome. Photios I of Constantinople describes him in his *Bibliotheca* **(cod. 121)** as a disciple of Irenaeus, who was said to be a disciple of Polycarp. He came into conflict with the popes of his time and seems to have headed a schismatic group as a rival bishop of Rome. For that reason he is sometimes considered the first Antipope. He opposed the Roman bishops who softened the penitential system to accommodate the large number of new pagan converts. However, he was very probably reconciled to the Church when he died as a martyr. He is the person usually understood to be meant by Saint Hippolytus.

Ignatius of Antioch-*Ignatius of Antioch,* also known as *Theophorus* meaning *"God-bearer"* (35 or 50-between 98 and 117 A.D.), was among the Apostolic Fathers, was the third Bishop and Patriarch of Antioch, and was a student of John the Apostle. While en route to Rome, Ignatius wrote a series of letters which have been preserved as an example of very early Christian theology. Important topics addressed in these letters include ecclesiology, the sacraments, and the role of bishops.

Irenaeus-*Saint Irenaeus,* (2nd century – 202 A.D.), was Bishop of Lugdunum in Gaul, then a part of the Roman Empire (now Lyons, France). He was an early church father and apologist, and his writings were formative in the early development of Christian theology. He was a hearer of Polycarp, who in turn was a disciple of John the Evangelist. Irenaeus' best-known book, *Adversus Haereses*or *Against Heresies* (180 A.D.) is a detailed attack on Gnosticism, which was then a serious threat to the Church, and especially on the system of the Gnostic Valentinus. As one of the first great Christian theologians, he emphasized the traditional elements in the Church. He was against the Gnostics, who said that they possessed a secret oral tradition from Jesus himself. Irenaeus maintained that the bishops in different cities are known as far back as the Apostles and none of them were Gnostics, and that the bishops provided the only safe guide to the interpretation of Scripture. His writings, with those of Clement and Ignatius, are taken to hint at papal primacy. Irenaeus is the earliest witness to recognition of the canonical character of all four gospels.

John the Apostle-*John the Apostle,* also known as *John the Beloved Disciple,* (6-100 A.D.), was one of the Twelve Apostles of Jesus. He was the son of Zebedee and Salome, and brother of James also the son of Zebedee, another of the Twelve Apostles. Christian tradition holds he was the last surviving of the Twelve Apostles, the only one to die a natural death and died around the age of 100. Christian tradition identifies him as the author of several New Testament works; the Gospel of John, the Epistles of John, and the Book of Revelation.

John the Baptist-*John the Baptist* was a preacher and a major religious figure that baptized Jesus Christ and led a movement of baptism at the Jordan River. John was a historical figure who followed the example of previous Hebrew prophets, living austerely, challenging sinful rulers, calling for repentance, and promising God's justice. John is regarded as a prophet in Christianity.

John Calvin-*John Calvin,* (July 10, 1509 –May 27, 1564 A.D.), was an influential French theologian and pastor during the Protestant Reformation. He was a principal figure in the development of the system of Christian theology later called Calvinism. Originally trained as a humanist lawyer, he broke from the Roman Catholic Church around 1530 A.D. After religious tensions provoked a violent uprising against Protestants in France, Calvin fled to Basel, Switzerland, where in 1536 A.D. he published the first edition of his seminal work *Institutes of the Christian Religion.*

John Gill-*John Gill,* (November 23, 1697 – October 14, 1771 A.D.), was an English Baptist, biblical scholar, "Jehovist", and held to a staunch Calvinistic Soteriology. Born in Kettering, Northamptonshire, he attended Kettering Grammar School where he mastered the Latin classics and learned Greek by age eleven. He continued self-study in everything from logic to Hebrew.

John Wycliffe-*John Wycliffe*; also spelled *Wyclif, Wycliff, Wiclef, Wicliffe,* or *Wickliffe,* (1324–December 31, 1384 A.D.), was an English theologian, lay preacher, translator, reformist and university teacher who was known as an early dissident in the Roman Catholic Church during the 14th century. His followers are known as Lollards, a somewhat rebellious movement, which preached anticlerical and biblically-centered reforms. He is considered the founder of the Lollard movement, a precursor to the Protestant Reformation, for this reason he is sometimes called *"The Morning Star of the Reformation".* He was one of the earliest opponents of papal authority influencing secular power. Wycliffe was also an early advocate for translation of the Bible into the common tongue. He completed his translation directly from the Vulgate into vernacular English in the year 1382 A.D., now known as Wyclif's Bible. It is probable that he personally translated the Gospels of Matthew, Mark, Luke, and John; and it is possible he translated the entire New Testament, while his associates translated the Old Testament. Wyclif's Bible appears to have been completed by 1384 A.D, with additional updated versions being done by Wycliffe's assistant John Purvey and others in 1388 A.D. and 1395 A.D.

Jose Luis De Jesus Miranda-*José Luis de Jesús Miranda,* (born April 22, 1946 in Ponce, Puerto Rico), is the founder and leader of *Creciendo en Gracia* (Growing In Grace International Ministry, Inc.), a movement that teaches the *"doctrine of Grace."* It is based in Miami, Florida. He claims to be both Jesus Christ returned and the Antichrist, and exhibits a *"666"* tattoo on his forearm. He has referred to himself as *"Jesucristo*

Hombre" which translates to *"The Man Christ Jesus"*. *Creciendo en Gracia* has been described as a cult by cult expert Rick Ross, and Freedom of Mind's Steven Hassan. In 2007 the *Dallas Morning News* reported that de Jesús "preaches to followers in some 35 nations, mostly in Latin America, and has 287 radio programs and a 24-hour Spanish-language TV network." De Jesús has gained attention in Puerto Rico in particular, where his denomination has opened centers in Guaynabo, Arecibo, Yabucoa, Ponce and Hormigueros. In early 2007 he acknowledged others' claims that he was the Antichrist and explained that the term is true. It applies because people are no longer to follow the *"Jewish teachings"* of Jesus of Nazareth, but rather to follow the Apostle Paul's teachings through de Jesús. According to de Jesús, *"Antichrist"* means *"no longer following Jesus of Nazareth as he lived in the days of his flesh"*. Followers have shown their support by getting *"666"* tattoos on their bodies. *"666"*, de Jesús explains, is not a sign of the Devil, because the Devil was destroyed, but the number of the Antichrist. De Jesús and his followers celebrate Christmas each year on April 22, as this is the day de Jesús was born and therefore they claim it is the *"real"* Christmas.

Josephus-*Josephus,* (37– 100 A.D.), also *Yosef Ben Matityahu (Joseph son of Matthias)* and *Titus Flavius Josephus* was a first-century Jewish historian who recorded first century Jewish history, such as the First Jewish–Roman War which resulted in the Destruction of Jerusalem in 70 A.D. He has been credited by many as recording some of the earliest history of Jesus Christ outside of the gospels. He lived a contemporary life with the apostles. Josephus was a law-observant Jew who believed in the compatibility of Judaism and Greco-Roman thought, commonly referred to as Hellenistic Judaism. His most important works were *The Jewish War* (75 A.D.) and *Antiquities of the Jews* (94 A.D.). *The Jewish War* recounts the Jewish revolt against Roman occupation (66–70 A.D.). *Antiquities of the Jews* recounts the history of the world from a Jewish perspective for a Roman audience. These works provide valuable insight into first century Judaism and the background of Early Christianity.

Justin Martyr-*Justin Martyr* (also *Justin the Martyr, Justin of Caesarea, Justin the Philosopher,* Latin *Iustinus Martyr* or *Flavius Iustinus*) (103–165 A.D.) was an early Christian apologist and saint. His works represent the earliest surviving Christian "apologies" of notable size. Most of what is known about the life of Justin Martyr comes from his own writings. He was born at Flavia Neapolis (ancient Shechem in Judaea/Palaestina, now modern-day Nablus). According to the traditional accounts of the church, Justin suffered martyrdom at Rome under the Emperor Marcus Aurelius when Junius Rusticus was prefect of the city (between 162 and 168 A.D.).

Kind David-*David* was the second king of the United Kingdom of Israel according to the Hebrew Bible. He is depicted as a righteous king, as well as an acclaimed warrior, musician and poet, traditionally credited for composing many of the psalms contained in the Book of Psalms. Edwin Thiele dates his life to 1040–970 B.C., his reign over Judah 1010–1003 B.C., and his reign over the United Kingdom of Israel 1003–970 B.C. The Books of Samuel, 1 Kings, and 1 Chronicles are the only source of information on his life and reign, although the Tel Dan stele records the existence in the mid-ninth century of a Judean royal dynasty called the *"House of David"*. David's life is particularly important to Jewish, Christian, and Islamic culture. In Judaism, David, or Melekh David, is the King of Israel, and the Jewish people. A direct descendant of David will be the Mashiach. In Christianity David is known as an ancestor of Jesus' adoptive father Joseph, and in Islam, he is considered to be a prophet and the king of a nation.

King Herod-*Herod,* also known as *Herod I* or *Herod the Great* (74- 4 B.C.), was an Edomite Jewish Roman client king of Israel. He was described as *"a madman who murdered his own family and a great many rabbis."* He is also known for his colossal building projects in Jerusalem and other parts of the ancient world, including the rebuilding of the Second Temple in Jerusalem, sometimes referred to as Herod's Temple. Some details of his biography can be gleaned from the works of the 1st century Roman-Jewish historian Josephus Flavius. His son Herod Antipas, who continued the Herodian dynasty, was ruler of Galilee (4 B.C. - 39 A.D.) during the time of John the Baptist and Jesus of Nazareth.

Louis A. Bowman-*Louis Bowman,* (1872-1959), was born in Illinois. In 1948, Bowman first inserted the phrase *"under God"* into the Pledge of Allegiance. He reportedly was inspired to make the change by Abraham Lincoln's use of *"under God"* in his Gettysburg Address.

Luke the Apostle-*Luke the Evangelist* was an Early Christian writer who the Church Fathers such as Jerome and Eusebius said was the author of the Gospel of Luke and the Acts of the Apostles The Roman Catholic Church venerates him as Saint Luke, patron saint of physicians, surgeons, students, butchers, and artists.

Madalyn Murray O'Hair-*Madalyn Murray O'Hair* (April 13, 1919 – September 29, 1995) was an American atheist activist, and founder of the organization American Atheists In 1960, Murray filed a lawsuit against the Baltimore City Public School System, in which she asserted that it was unconstitutional for her son William to be required to participate in Bible readings at Baltimore public schools. In this litigation, she stated that her son's refusal to partake in the Bible readings had resulted in bullying being directed against him by classmates, and that administrators condoned this. After consolidation with *Abington School District v. Schempp,* the lawsuit reached the Supreme Court of the United States in 1963. The Court voted 8-1 in Murray's favor, which effectively banned coercive prayer and Bible verse recitation at public schools in the United States. Thereafter, she declared herself to have been the leader of the movement to remove prayer from public schools. However, her son William later noted that there were several similar cases before the Supreme Court at the same time, and her case simply happened to be decided first.

Mark the Apostle-_Mark the Apostle_ was a companion of Saint Paul in Acts, who later is said to have become a companion of Saint Peter. About ten to twenty years after the ascension of Christ, Saint Mark traveled to Alexandria and founded the Church of Alexandria, which today is the Coptic Orthodox Church. Aspects of the Coptic liturgy can be traced back to Saint Mark himself. He became the first bishop of Alexandria and he is honored as the founder of Christianity in Africa. He died in the eighth year of Nero and was buried there.

Martin Luther-_Martin Luther,_ (November 10, 1483– February 18, 1546 A.D.) was a German priest and professor of theology who initiated the Protestant Reformation. Strongly disputing the claim that freedom from God's punishment of sin could be purchased with money, he confronted indulgence salesman Johann Tetzel with his _Ninety-Five Theses_ in 1517 A.D. His refusal to retract all of his writings at the demand of Pope Leo X in 1520 A.D. and the Holy Roman Emperor Charles V at the Diet of Worms in 1521 A.D. resulted in his excommunication by the pope and condemnation as an outlaw by the emperor. Luther taught that salvation is not earned by good deeds but received only as a free gift of God's grace through faith in Jesus as redeemer from sin. His theology challenged the authority of the pope of the Roman Catholic Church by teaching that the Bible is the only source of divinely revealed knowledge and opposed sacerdotalism by considering all baptized Christians to be a holy priesthood. Those who identify with Luther's teachings are called Lutherans.

Marvin Meyer-_Marvin Meyer_ is a scholar of religion and a professor at Chapman University, in Orange, California. He is also Director of the Coptic Magical Texts Project of the Institute for Antiquity and Christianity. Dr. Meyer is the author of numerous books and articles on Greco-Roman and Christian religions in antiquity. Meyer is best known for his translations of the texts of documents associated with the ancient mystery religions, early Christian magic, and Gnostic texts, of which the most notable have been the Gospel of Thomas and the Gospel of Judas. He is regarded as an authority on Gnosticism and has published many books on the subject

Matthew the Apostle-*Matthew the Evangelist,* (*"Gift of Yahweh"*, Standard Hebrew and Tiberian Hebrew: *Mattay* or *Mattithyahu*; Septuagint Greek: *Matthaios*) was one of the twelve Apostles of Jesus and one of the four Evangelists. Matthew, a former tax collector, composed the *Gospel of Christ*. It was first published in Judea in Hebrew for Hebrew Christians. It was later translated into Greek. In addition, the Gospel according to the Hebrews is alleged to have been written by Matthew as well.

Matthew Henry-*Matthew Henry,* (October 18, 1662 – June 22, 1714 A.D), was an English commentator on the Bible and Presbyterian minister. He gave up his legal studies for theology, and in 1687 A.D. he became minister of a Presbyterian congregation at Chester. He moved again in 1712 A.D. to Mare Street, Hackney. Two years later (June 22, 1714), he died suddenly while on a journey from Chester to London.

Nero-*Nero Claudius Caesar Augustus Germanicus,* (December 15, 37 – June 9, 68 A.D.), born *Lucius Domitius Ahenobarbus*, and also called *Nero Claudius Caesar Drusus Germanicus.* He was Roman Emperor from 54- 68 A.D., and was the last of the Julio-Claudian dynasty. Nero was adopted by his great-uncle Claudius to become heir to the throne. He succeeded to the throne in 54 A.D. following Claudius' death. He is also infamously known as the emperor who *"fiddled while Rome burned"*, and as an early persecutor of Christians. This view is based upon the main surviving sources for Nero's reign - Tacitus, Suetonius and Cassius Dio.

Origen-*Origen,* (Greek: *Ōrigénēs,* or *Origen Adamantius,* 185–254 A.D.), was an early Christian scholar and theologian, and one of the most distinguished writers of the early Christian Church despite not being considered a Church father by some. According to tradition, he is thought to have been an Egyptian who taught in Alexandria. The patriarch of Alexandria at first supported Origen but later expelled him for being ordained without the patriarch's permission. He relocated to Caesarea Maritima and died there after being tortured during a persecution.

Pelagius-*Pelagius,* (354 –420/440 A.D.), was an ascetic who denied the doctrine of original sin as developed by Augustine of Hippo, and was declared a heretic by the Council of Carthage. His interpretation of a doctrine of free will became known as *Pelagianism.* He was well educated, fluent in both Greek and Latin, and learned in theology.

Peter of Alexandria-was Pope of Alexandria (300 – 311-12 A.D.). He is revered as a saint by the Coptic Orthodox Church, the Roman Catholic Church, and the Eastern Orthodox Church Peter's time as bishop included the most terrible persecution Christianity was subjected to, that of Roman Emperor Diocletian, which began in 303, and continued intermittently over the next ten years.

Peter the Apostle-*Simon Peter,* (Greek: Πέτρος, *Pétros, "stone, rock";* 1 B.C. – 67 A.D.), sometimes called *Simon Cephas,* was a leader of the early Christian Church, who is featured prominently in the New Testament Gospels and the Acts of the Apostles. Peter was the son of John or of Jonah, and was from the village of Bethsaida in the province of Galilee. His brother Andrew was also an apostle. Simon Peter is venerated in multiple churches and regarded as the first Pope by the Roman Catholic Church.

Phillip the Apostle-*Saint Philip the Apostle,* (Greek: Φιλιππος, *Philippos*) was one of the Twelve Apostles of Jesus. Later Christian traditions describe Philip as the apostle who preached in Greece, Syria, and Phrygia. Gnostic Christians appealed to the apostolic authority of Philip, ascribing a number of Gnostic texts to him, most notably the Gospel of Philip from the Nag Hammadi library.

Pliny the Younger-*Gaius Plinius Caecilius Secundus*, born *Gaius Caecilius* or *Gaius Caecilius Cilo* (61 A.D. –112 A.D.), better known as *Pliny the Younger*, was a lawyer, author, and magistrate of Ancient Rome. Pliny is known for his hundreds of surviving letters, which are an invaluable historical source for the period. Many are addressed to reigning emperors or to notables such as the historian, Tacitus.

Polycrates of Ephesus-*Polycrates of Ephesus* (130 - 196 A.D.) was an Early Christian leader who resided in Ephesus. He should not be confused with Polycrates of Samos. Roberts and Donaldson noted that Polycrates *"belonged to a family in which he was the eighth Christian bishop; and he presided over the church of Ephesus, in which the traditions of St. John were yet fresh in men's minds at the date of his birth. He had doubtless known Polycarp, and Irenaeus also. He seems to have presided over a synod of Asiatic bishops (A.D. 196) which came together to consider this matter of the Paschal feast. It is surely noteworthy that nobody doubted that it was kept by a Christian and Apostolic ordinance. So St. Paul argues from its Christian observance, in his rebuke of the Corinthians. They were keeping it 'unleavened' ceremonially, and he urges a spiritual unleavening as more important. The Christian hallowing of Pentecost connects with the Paschal (Passover over Easter) argument. The Christian Sabbath hinges on these points."*- **The Ante-Nicene Fathers, 1885**

Pontius Pilate-*Pontius Pilate* (Latin: *Pontius Pilatus*), was the fifth Prefect of the Roman province of Judaea from 26–36 A.D. He is best known as the judge at Jesus' trial and the man who authorized his crucifixion. Pilate appears in all four canonical Christian Gospels. In Matthew, Pilate washes his hands of Jesus and reluctantly sends him to his death. Mark, depicting Jesus as innocent of plotting against Rome, portrays Pilate as extremely reluctant to execute Jesus, blaming the Jewish priestly hierarchy for his death. In Luke, Pilate not only agrees that Jesus did not conspire against Rome, but Herod Antipas, the tetrarch, also finds nothing treasonable in Jesus' actions.

Pope Damascus-*Pope Saint Damascus I,* was Pope from 366-384 A.D. He was born around 305 A.D., probably near the city of Idanha-a-Velha (in Lusitania, Hispania); in what is present-day Portugal, then part of the Western Roman Empire. His life coincided with the rise of Constantine I and the reunion and re-division of the Western and Eastern Roman Empires, associated with the widespread legitimization of Christianity and the later adoption of Christianity as the religion of the Roman state.

Pope Leo X-*Pope Leo X,* (December 11, 1475 –December 1, 1521 A.D.), was Pope from 1513 to his death in 1521 A.D. He was the last non-priest to be elected Pope. He is known primarily for the sale of indulgences to reconstruct St. Peter's Basilica and his challenging of Martin Luther's 95 page theses. He was the second son of Lorenzo de' Medici, the most famous ruler of the Florentine Republic, and Clarice Orsini. His cousin, Giulio di Giuliano de' Medici, would later succeed him as Pope Clement VII (1523–34 A.D.).

Pope St. John-*Pope St. John,* 53rd pope in 523 A.D. Italy's ruler, Theodoric the Goth, was an Arian. For a while he let Catholics alone, but in later life became suspicious of everyone, imagining conspiracies and attempts to seize his throne. He tried to involve Pope John in his political machinations. John led a delegation to Constantinople to negotiate with Emperor Justin I; he was the first pope to travel to Constantinople, and while there crowned Justin. The mission was successful, but Theodoric thought John and Justin I had plotted against him. While returning to Rome, John was kidnapped and imprisoned by Theodoric's soldiers; he died in custody.

Praxeas-*Praxeas* was a Monarchian from Asia Minor who lived in the end of the 2nd century/beginning of the 3rd century. He believed in the unity of the Godhead and disagreed with any attempt at division of the personalities or personages of the Father, Son, and Holy Spirit in the Christian Church. He was opposed by Tertullian in his tract, *Against Praxeas (Adversus Praxean).*

Priscillian-*Priscillian* (died 385 A.D.) was bishop of Ávila and a theologian from Roman Gallaecia (in the Iberian Peninsula), the first person in the history of Christianity to be executed for heresy (though the civil charges were for the practice of magic). He founded an ascetic group that, in spite of persecution, continued to subsist in Hispania and Gaul until the late 6th century. Tractates by Priscillian and close followers, which had seemed certainly lost, were recovered in 1885 and published in 1889.

René Descartes-*René Descartes,* (March 31, 1596 –February 11, 1650 A.D.), was a French philosopher, mathematician, physicist, and writer who spent most of his adult life in the Dutch Republic. He has been dubbed the *"Father of Modern Philosophy",* and much of subsequent Western philosophy is a response to his writings, which continue to be studied closely to this day. In particular, his *Meditations on First Philosophy* continues to be a standard text at most university philosophy departments.

Sabellius-*Sabellius* was a third century priest and theologian who most likely taught in Rome, but may have been an African from Libya. Sabellius taught that God was indivisible, with Father, Son, and Holy Spirit being three modes or manifestations of one divine Person. A Sabellian modalist would say that the One God successively revealed Himself to man throughout time as the Father in Creation; the Son in Redemption; and the Spirit in Sanctification and Regeneration.

Sextus Julius Africanus-*Sextus Julius Africanus,* (160-240 A.D.), was a Christian traveler and historian of the late second and early third century A.D. He is important chiefly because of his influence on Eusebius, on all the later writers of Church history among the Fathers. His name indicates that he was an African. Suidas calls him *"a Libyan philosopher",* while Gelzer considers him of Roman descent. Julius called himself a native of Jerusalem – which some scholars consider his birthplace – and lived at the neighboring Emmaus He wrote a history of the world (*Chronographiai,* in five books) from Creation to the year 221 A.D., covering, according to his computation, 5723 years. He calculated the period between Creation and Jesus as 5500 years, placing the Incarnation on the first day of 5501. (March 25, 1 B.C.). This method of reckoning led to several Creation eras being used in the Greek Eastern Mediterranean, which all placed Creation within one decade of 5500 B.C. He was the first church writer to give the date of December twenty-fifth as the birthday of Jesus in 221 A.D.

Simon of Cyrene-*Simon of Cyrene* was the person compelled by the Romans to carry the cross of Jesus, according to all three Synoptic Gospels According to some Gnostic traditions, Simon of Cyrene, by mistaken identity, suffered the events leading up to the crucifixion, and died on the cross instead of Jesus.

Simon Magus-*Simon Magus,* also known as *Simon the Sorcerer* and *Simon of Gitta,* was a Samaritan proto-Gnostic and traditional founder of the *Simonians* in the first century A.D. His only Biblical reference is in **Acts 8:9-24** and prominently in several apocryphal and some early Christian writers, some of whom regarded him as the source of all heresies, particularly St. Justin who wrote about Simon about one hundred years after his life. His followers referred to him as the *Great Power of God.* There were later accusations by Christians that he was a demon in human form, and he was specifically said to possess the ability to levitate and fly at will.

St. Alexander-*Saint Alexander of Constantinople*, (born between 237 and 244 – 337 A.D.), was bishop of Byzantium and the bishop of Constantinople (the city was renamed during his episcopacy). From a very young age he was given to God and stayed in a Monastery, where he cultivated virtue and became a good laborer of God's commands.

St. Ambrose-*Aurelius Ambrosius*, better known in English as *Saint Ambrose* (337–April 4, 397 A.D.), was a bishop of Milan who became one of the most influential ecclesiastical figures of the fourth century. He is counted as one of the four original doctors of the Church.

St. Basil the Great-*Basil of Caesarea*, (330 – January 1, 379 A.D.), was the bishop of Caesarea Mazaca in Cappadocia, Asia Minor (modern-day Turkey). He was an influential forth century Christian theologian and monastic. Basil was a supporter of the Nicene faction of the church, in opposition to Aryanism on one side and the followers of Apollinaris of Laodicea on the other. His ability to balance his theological convictions with his political connections made Basil a powerful advocate for the Nicene position

St. Cyril of Alexandria-*Cyril of Alexandria*, (376 – 444 A.D.), was the Pope of Alexandria from 412-444 A.D. He came to power when the city was at its height of influence and power within the Roman Empire. Cyril wrote extensively and was a leading protagonist in the Christological controversies of the later fourth and fifth centuries. He was a central figure in the First Council of Ephesus in 431 A.D., which led to the deposition of Nestorius as Patriarch of Constantinople. Cyril is counted among the Church Fathers and the Doctors of the Church, and his reputation within the Christian world has resulted in his titles *Pillar of Faith* and *Seal of all the Fathers*, but Theodosius II, the Roman Emperor, condemned him for behaving like a *proud pharaoh*, and the Nestorian bishops at the Council of Ephesus declared him a heretic, labeling him as a *"monster, born and educated for the destruction of the church"*.

St. Jerome-*Saint Jerome,* (347 – September 30, 420 A.D.) (Latin: *Eusebius Sophronius Hieronymus*), was an Illyrian Christian priest and apologist. He was the son of Eusebius, of the city of Stridon, which was on the border of Dalmatia and Pannoni (and was overthrown by the Goths). He is best known for his new translation of the Bible into Latin, which has since come to be called the Vulgate and his list of writings are extensive. He is recognized by the Catholic Church as a saint and Doctor of the Church and his version of the Bible is still an important text in Catholicism. He is also recognized as a saint by the Eastern Orthodox Church, where he is known as *St. Jerome of Stridonium* or *Blessed Jerome.*

St. Fulgentius of Ruspe-*Saint Fulgentius of Ruspe,* (462 or 467 —January 1, 527 or 533 A.D.), was bishop of the city of Ruspe, North Africa, in the fifth and sixth century who was canonized as a Christian saint. *Fabius Claudius Gordianus Fulgentius* was born into a noble family of Carthage. As a theologian, Fulgentius's work shows knowledge of Greek and a strong agreement with Augustine of Hippo. He wrote frequently against Arianism and Pelagianism. Some letters and eight sermons survive by Fulgentius.

St. John-*John Chrysostom,* (349-407 A.D.), Archbishop of Constantinople, was an important Early Church Father. He is known for his eloquence in preaching and public speaking, his denunciation of abuse of authority by both ecclesiastical and political leaders, the Divine Liturgy of St. John Chrysostom, and his ascetic sensibilities. After his death he was given the Greek surname *chrysostomos,* meaning *"golden mouthed",* rendered in English as Chrysostom.

St. Paul-*Paul of Tarsus,* also called *Paul the Apostle,* the *Apostle Paul,* and *Saint Paul,* (Ancient Greek: Σαούλ *Saul, Saulos,* and *Paulos*); Latin: *Paulus* or *Paullus;* (5 -67 A.D.), was a Jew who referred to himself as the "Apostle to the Gentiles," (in **Romans 1:13**). According to the Acts of the Apostles, his conversion to faith in Jesus took place in a profound life-changing experience on the road to Damascus. Together with Simon Peter and James the Just, he is considered among the most notable of early Christian leaders. He was also a Roman Citizen, a fact that afforded him a privileged legal status with respect to laws, property, and governance. Thirteen epistles in the New Testament are traditionally attributed to Paul, of which seven are almost universally accepted, three are considered in some academic circles as other than Pauline for textual and grammatical reasons, and the other three are in dispute in those same circles. Paul apparently dictated all his epistles through a secretary (or amanuensis), who would usually paraphrase the gist of his message, as was the practice among first-century scribes. These epistles were circulated within the Christian community, where they were read aloud by members of the church along with other works. Paul's epistles were accepted early as scripture and later established as Canon of Scripture. Critical scholars regard Paul's epistles (written 50-62 A.D.) to be the earliest-written books of the New Testament.

Suetonius-_Gaius Suetonius Tranquillus,_ commonly known as _Suetonius_ (69/75 – after 130 A.D.), was an equestrian and a historian during the Roman Empire. His most important surviving work is a set of biographies of twelve successive Roman rulers, from Julius Caesar until Domitian, entitled _De Vita Caesarum._ Other works by Suetonius concern the daily life of Rome, politics, oratory, and the lives of famous writers, including poets, historians, and grammarians. A few of these books have partially survived, but many are entirely lost.

Tacitus-_Publius_ (or _Gaius_) _Cornelius Tacitus,_ (56 –117 A.D.), was a senator and a historian of the Roman Empire. The surviving portions of his two major works—the _Annals_ and the _Histories_—examine the reigns of the Roman Emperors Tiberius, Claudius, Nero and those who reigned in the Year of the Four Emperors. These two works span the history of the Roman Empire from the death of Augustus in 14 A.D.to the death of Emperor Domitian in 96 A.D. He is one of the few anti-Christians who mention Christ.

Tertullian-_Quintus Septimius Florens Tertullianus_, anglicised as _Tertullian_ (160–220 A.D.), was a prolific early Christian author from Carthage in the Roman province of Africa. He is the first Christian author to produce an extensive corpus of Latin Christian literature. He also was a notable early Christian apologist and a polemicist against heresy. Tertullian has been called _"the father of Lati Christianity"_. Though conservative; he did originate and advance new theology to the early Church. He is perhaps most famous for being the oldest extant Latin writer to use the term Trinity (Latin trinitas), and giving the oldest extant formal exposition of a Trinitarian theology. Other Latin formulations that first appear in his work are _"three Persons, one Substance"_ as the Latin _"tres Personae, una Substantia"_ (itself from the Koine Greek "treis Hypostases, Homoousios"). Some of Tertullian's ideas were not acceptable to the Orthodox Church; in later life he became a Montanist renouncing Catholicism. Montanism was an early Christian movement of the early second century, named after its founder Montanus. It is still part of Christianity, despite of internet rumors of him renouncing his Christianity, but not accepted by the mainstream Orthodox Church. Tertullian did not agree with the direction of the early church. He did believe that the new prophecy was genuine and began to fall out of step with what he began to call _"the church of a lot of bishops."_ The practice of maontanism was later considered as heresy.

Thomas Pain-_Thomas "Tom" Paine,_ (February 9, 1737 – June 8, 1809), was an author, pamphleteer, radical, inventor, intellectual, revolutionary, and one of the Founding Fathers of the United States. He has been called _"a corset maker"_ by trade, a journalist by profession, and a propagandist by inclination."

Titus Flavius Vespasianus-*Titus Flavius Vespasianus* (December 30, 39 – September 13, 81 A.D.), commonly known as **Titus**, was Roman Emperor from 79 to 81 A.D. A member of the Flavian dynasty, Titus succeeded his father Vespasian upon his death. Despite concerns over his character, Titus ruled to great acclaim following the death of Vespasian in 79, and was considered a good emperor by Suetonius and other contemporary historians. As emperor, he is best known for completing the Colosseum and for his generosity in relieving the suffering caused by two disasters, the Mount Vesuvius eruption of 79 and a fire in Rome in 80.

Trajan-*Marcus Ulpius Nerva Traianus,* (September 18, 53 – August 9, 117 A.D.), was Roman Emperor from 98-117 A.D.

William Tyndale-*William Tyndale* (sometimes spelled *Tindall* or *Tyndall*; (1494 – 1536 A.D.), was a 16th century scholar and translator who became a leading figure in Protestant reformism towards the end of his life. He was influenced by the work of Desiderius Erasmus, who made the Greek New Testament available in Europe, and Martin Luther. Tyndale was the first to translate considerable parts of the Bible into English. While a number of partial and complete translations had been made from the seventh century onward, particularly during the fourteenth century, Tyndale's was the first English translation to draw directly from Hebrew and Greek texts, and the first to take advantage of the new medium of print, which allowed for its wide distribution. This was taken to be a direct challenge to the hegemony of both the Catholic Church and the English church. In 1535 A.D., Tyndale was arrested by church authorities and jailed in the castle of Vilvoorde outside Brussels for over a year. He was tried for heresy, strangled and burnt at the stake. The heretical Tyndale Bible, as it was known, continued to play a key role in spreading Reformation ideas across Europe.

Zephyrinus-*Pope Saint Zephyrinus,* born in Rome, was bishop of Rome from 199-217 A.D. His predecessor was Bishop Victor I. Upon his death on December 20, 217 A.D., he was succeeded by his principal advisor, bishop Callixtus I. Under Zephyrinus, the position of the Christians, which had remained favorable in the first years of the government of Emperor Septimius Severus (193–211 A.D.), grew constantly worse, and in 202 or 203 A.D. the edict of persecution appeared which forbade conversion to Christianity under the severest penalties.

The vast majority of the previous text came from Wikipedia.com.

Books of the Bible (KJV)

Old Testament	New Testament
Genesis	Matthew
Exodus	Mark
Leviticus	Luke
Numbers	John
Deuteronomy	Acts of the Apostles
Joshua	Romans
Judges	I Corinthians
Ruth	II Corinthians
I Samuel	Galatians
II Samuel	Ephesians
I Kings	Phillipians
II Kings	Colossians
I Chronicles	I Thessalonians
II Chronicles	II Thessalonians
Ezra	I Timothy
Nehemiah	II Timothy
Ester	Titus
Job	Philemon
Psalms	Hebrews
Proverbs	James

Ecclesiastes

Song of Solomon

Isaiah

Jeremiah

Lamentations

Ezekiel

Daniel

Hosea

Joel

Amos

Obadiah

Jonah

Micah

Nahum

Habakkuk

Zephaniah

Haggai

Zechariah

Malachi

I Peter

II Peter

I John

II John

III John

Jude

Revelation

Bible versions

Jerome	347-420
New Testament Translation	733
John Wycliffe	1324-1384
Alcala Polyglot Bible of Cardinal Ximenes	1514-1517
Tyndale's New Testament	1534
Coverdale's Bible	1534
Matthew's Bible	1537
Taverner's Bible	1539
Great Bible	1539

Geneva Bible	1560
Bishop's Bible	1568
Reina Valera	1569
Rheims New Testament	1582
Sixtus Latin Vulgate	1590
The Authorized Catholic Latin Vulgate	1592
Douay-Rheims	1609
King James Version	1611
Young's Literal Translation	1862
Emphasized Bible	1878
The New King James Version	1882-1884
Weymouth New Testament	1890
American Standard Version	1901
Worrell New Testament	1904
American Translation	NT 1923 OT 1927

Montgomery New Testament	1924
Moffatt Bible	1926
Lamsa Bible	1933
Modern Language Bible	1945
New World Translation	1950
Revised Standard Version	1952
Amplified Bible: New Testament	1958
New Testament in Modern English	1947
Wuest Expanded Translation New Testament	1956
New American Standard Bible	1960
New English Bible	1961
Amplified Bible: Old Testament	1965
Good News Version	1966
Jerusalem Bible	1966

New Life Bible	1969
The New American Bible	1970
The Living Bible	1971
The New International Version	1973
English Version for the Deaf	1978
Simple English Version	1980
The Schoken Bible Volume 1: The 5 Books of Moses	1983
New Jerusalem Bible	1985
The Jewish Translation, Tanach	1985
Biblia de las Americas	1986
New Century Version	1987
God's Word	1988
Revised English Bible	1989
Jewish New Testament	1989

New Revised Standard Version	1990
Contemporary English Version	NT 1990 OT 1995
Good News Bible	1992
Alba House Bible	1992
The Black Bible Chronicles	1993
Twenty-first Century King James Version	1994
New International Reader's Version	1996
Richmond Lattimore Translation of the New Testament	1996
New Living Translation	1996
English Standard Version	2001
Holman Christian Standard Bible	2001
The Message	2002

Study Bibles

Life Application Bible
Full Life Study Bible
Rainbow Study Bible
Original African Heritage Bible
One Year Bible
Harper Collins Study Bible with Apocrypha
New Oxford Annotated Bible
Parallel Reina-Valera (1960) and KJVD
Parallel Reina-Valera (1960) and NIVB
From Genesis to the Promise Land
Men's Devotional Bible
New Adventure Bible
NIV Study Bible
Women's Devotional Bible
Young Explorer's Study Bible
Life Application Bible for Students
Spirit Filled Life Study bible

Bibliography

Anderson, Ken. 1996. *Where to find it in the Bible.* Nashville, TN: Thomas Nelson.

Baigent, Michael. 2006. *The Jesus Papers.* New York, NY. HarperCollins.

Barton, David. 2008 *Original Intent,* 5th Edition. Aledo, TX: WallBuilder Press.

Baucham, Voddie Jr. 2007 *Family Driven Faith.* Wheaton, IL: Crossway Books.

Encyclopaedia Britannica, Inc. 15th Edition. 1975. The University of Chicago.

Brunt, P.A.& Moore J.M. 1990 *RES GESTAE DIVINE AUGUSTI.* Great Britain: J.W. Arrowsmith Ltd., Bristol

Clement of Alexandria. *The Miscellanies,* trans. William Wilson, 2 vols. Edinburgh, 1867, 1869 (Anti-Nicene Christian Library, vols. IV AND XII).

Cumont, Franz. 2007 *The Mysteries of Mithra,* Seond Revised Edition. San Diego, California: The Book Tree

Eadie, John. 1850 *Concordance to the Holy Scriptures, Cruden Condensed* 14th English Edition. New York, NY: American Tract Society.

Eusebius. 1981 *The History of the Church,* trans. G.A. William. Harmondsworth.

Everitt, Anthony. 2006 *Augustus*

Hippolytus. 1921 *Philoshumena, or The Refutation of all Heresies,* trans. F. Legge, 2 vols. London

Irenaeus of Lyons. 1868-9 *Against Heresies*. In The Writing of Irenaeus, trans. Alexander Roberts and W.H. Rambaut, 2 vols. Edinburgh.

Josephus, Flavius. 1978 *The Antiquities of the Jews*, trans. William Whiston. London, nd.

Livius, Titus. 1905 *The History of Rome,* trans. Rev. Canon Roberts, 6 vols. London

Farrer J.A. 1910 *Paganism and Christianity*. London: Watts&Co.,

Martyr, Justin. 1867 *Dialogue with Trypho*. In *The Writing of Justin Martyr and Athenagoras,* trans. Marcus Dods, George Reith, and B.P. Pratten. Edinburghr.

Messaros, Rev. Waldon. 1888 *The Road to Heaven, Christianity&Paganism*. Phild'a, PA: GlobeBible Publishers Co.,

Meyer, Marvin. 2005 *The Gnostic Gospels.*

McCabe, Joseph. 1943 *How Christianity grew out of Paganism*. Girard, Kansas: Haldeman-Julius Publications.

Notovich, Nicholas 2008 *The Unknown Life of Jesus Christ.*

Pliny. 1938-42 *Natural History,* trans. H. Rackham and W.H.S. Jones, 10 vols, London.

Tacitus, 1979 *The Annals of Imperial Rome,* trans. Michael Grant. Harmondsworth.

Tertullian. 1869 *The Writings of Tertullian*, 3 vols., ed Rev. Alexander Roberts and James Donaldson. Ante-Nicene Library, vol. XI, XV,XVIII. Edinburgh.

Tichenor, Henry. 1916 *The Creed of Constantine.*

Thomas Nelson Bibles. 2003 *The Holy Bible Authorized King James Version.* Thomas Nelson, Inc.

The Watch Tower Bible and Tract Society of Pennsylvania. 2009 *What Does the Bible Really Teach?* Brooklyn, NY: Watchtower Bible and Tract Society of New York, Inc.

Webster's New Ideal Dictionary. 1978 G. & C. Merriam Co.

Woods, Len. 2008 *Handbook of World Religions*. Uhrichsville, OH: Barbour Publishing, Inc.

Websites

www.accurapid.com

www.allaboutjesuschrist.org

www.alternate.org

www.angelfire.com

www.bible.org

www.bibleicalhebrew.com

www.bibleicalchronology.com

www.biblegateway.com

www.bibletruths.net

www.blueletterbible.org

www.christiandefense.org

www.christanity today.com

www.clarifyingchristianity.com

www.crivoice.org

www.cynus-study.com

www.dailycatholic.org

www.earlychristianwritings.com

www.eternalchristmass.com

www.focusonJerusalem.com

www.gci.org

www.geocities.com

www.gospelway.com

www.greatsite.com

www.harvardhouse.com

www.ichtus.info

www.jesus-messiah.com

www.jesuswalk.com

www.keyway.ca

www.midwestsugustinians.org

www.pbs.org

www.popesonparade.com

www.raturechrist.com
www.religioustolerance.org
ww.rickross.com
www.rogershermansociety,org
www.sullivan-country.com
www.theholidayspot.com
www.theopedia.com
www.touregypt.net
www.towerwatch.com

About the Author

I am a native of Louisiana where I have lived for 30 years. I currently act as Vice-Chairman and Deacon of my church in Slidell, La. From my early youth attending private Christian schools to my later adult life, I have always questioned the meaning of being a Christian. I have personally seen most divisions of Christianity in action, attended a large variety of churches, and Bible study classes with Christian minorities. With all I've seen and learned, I kept having the same unanswered questions come up inside me. What is the real meaning, and why are there so many different faiths and practices? Surely everyone cannot be right in what they truly believe and preach, so what is going on? After several years of personal study and growth I uncovered answers that I believe shed some light on my confusions and doubt. Information that would also help other Christians who may have felt the same as I did when I was lost to the truth. This personal trip into uncovering the truth of Christianity has strengthened my faith and built within me confidences I have never known or felt at any time in my life. I believe the truth must be known to knock down walls that have built around Christian sects dividing the faith and splitting the population into lost and confused Christians with little hope of salvation. My journey will continue to uncover more truths and break down the barriers that some Christians have built to protect themselves from insecurity. It is time to move outside the Christian box and into a new world in which all Christians can believe and practice their faith in a uniform matter that is consistent with the real teaching of Jesus.